# gropius

# gropius

**Alberto Busignani**

**Hamlyn**

London    New York    Sydney    Toronto

twentieth-century masters
General editors: H. L. Jaffé and A. Busignani

© copyright in the text G. C. Sansoni, Florence, 1972
© copyright this edition The Hamlyn Publishing Group Limited 1973
London · New York · Sydney · Toronto
Hamlyn House, Feltham, Middlesex, England
ISBN 0 600 33813 4

Filmset by: Photoprint Plates Limited, Rayleigh, Essex
Printed in Italy by: Industria Grafica L'Impronta, Scandicci, Florence
Bound in Italy by: Poligrafici Il Resto del Carlino, Bologna

**Distributed in the United States of America by Crown Publishers Inc.**

# contents

# List of colour plates

# List of black-and-white illustrations

Walter Gropius, who, taken all in all, is probably the most important architect of modern Europe, worked as senior assistant in the office of Peter Behrens from 1907 to 1910, when Behrens was designing and building the Turbine Factory for the Allgemeine Elektrizitäts-Gesellschaft, the AEG, of Berlin. This was the first time in which the new principles of industrial building appeared in an exact and rational form.

In 1907 Gropius was just twenty-four and had spent the previous five years studying architecture at the universities of Berlin and Munich, although he had not taken his degree. Anyone who wishes to examine the background and development of his work must of course consider this early and extremely fortunate experience in Behrens's office; an experience that was very soon to show an influence upon his own work. It was only four years later, in 1911, that Gropius designed the Fagus Works at Alfeld near Hanover, an incredibly fine building from which all the rest of his rational ideas evolved.

The fact that Behrens's work so soon showed an effect on Gropius's own makes one suppose that when he chose to start his work as an architect with Behrens it was, in fact, because he already had a very definite understanding of what Behrens was doing, as well as a mature realisation of his own objectives and ideas. Of course, to have assisted at the planning of the Turbine Factory must have been wonderfully stimulating for Gropius, but his architectural ideas could not have matured so quickly unless they had already existed, not merely as attitudes but as convictions, when he began working for Behrens. When they met, Gropius's plans were probably already as clear and positive as those of Behrens, if not more so; otherwise it would be hard to explain how he came to build anything as miraculously successful as the Fagus Works. Pevsner has written of this: 'Its plan quite clearly goes beyond that of Behrens for the AEG. Only a few details in the windows show the influence of Behrens. In the main part of the building, everything is new and full of brilliant ideas. For the first time the entire façade is of glass, with the supporting elements reduced to narrow strips of steel. There are no supports at the corners, an idea that was to be imitated several times later. The form of the flat roof is also changed. Only in Loos's buildings, some years before the Fagus Works, is there the same use of the absolute cube. Behrens's moderate balance between the horizontal and the vertical has been abandoned. Here, a thrusting horizontal movement, which is extremely effective, dominates the composition.'

In order to understand what Gropius, while still under thirty, had achieved, we must consider his earlier history. From 1906 to 1909, before he met

Pls. 1–4 Figs. 1–3

Behrens, he was working on plans for some farm labourers' houses at Janikow in Pomerania. Already, in this first work of his, he seems to have renounced all attempts to find a particular style, and to have chosen instead a design of such bare simplicity that, at the time and even later, it might have been mistaken for non-art, suited to the modest purpose of the job—in other words, the building of labourers' houses. Yet here already, the lack of any stylistic superstructure, apart from that demanded by the bare necessity of the structure, could be seen as deliberate and rational: later this would be developed in the Fagus Works.

The subject is revealing, too. Quite clearly, Gropius was already interested in a socially responsible form of architecture. In this, his earliest work, he built workers' houses; then he went on to industrial buildings that would make essential changes in the workers' surroundings; and from this it was only a short step to the social ideas of the Bauhaus. In 1910, Gropius made a suggestion to Rathenau, president of the AEG, which was significant: he suggested setting up a firm to build houses from prefabricated and standardised elements. This idea not only brilliantly foresaw the role that industry could and should play in architecture, but also showed Gropius's basic preoccupation with equality in living standards; a kind of architectural socialism that was particularly valuable in pre-war Germany, dominated, as it was, by the industrial power of its highly traditional middle class.

1 Alfeld an der Leine. Fagus Works, 1911.

The date of this building—1911—is important. It is all too easy to forget how early it was, and to think of it as belonging to the post-war period in Germany, where it seems to belong. It is, indeed, in the Utopian atmosphere of the Weimar Republic, when German intellectuals were seeking to counterbalance the mistakes of the upper middle classes, on which weighed the responsibility for the war, that the social ideas of the Fagus Works seem to belong; but again it would be wrong to think that Germany had purged itself of its old errors, either politically or historically. It was this same upper middle class that was to deliver the country into the power of the Nazis, and later into disaster even more terrible; and thus to exile its intellectuals, including Gropius, who was among the first to suffer as a result of the intolerance of the ruling classes, with the closing of the Bauhaus in Weimar in 1925. Today, we know that far more radical changes were needed; for effective, sound measures to be taken, working-class support for them was indispensible, whereas, in fact, the new and rather dangerously Utopian ideas came from an enlightened industrial middle class, with the determined support of the intellectuals.

However this may be, the date of the Fagus Works, 1911, undoubtedly indicates what Gropius's social and architectural beliefs were at the time; and in the critical post-war years he was ready to try to save whatever possible through rational ideas which were completely positive, technically

2 Alfeld an der Leine.
Fagus Works, 1911.

viable, and free from sentiment. These ideas were rooted in a world that was, as we now know, moving towards another war, but at the time seemed healthy, and indeed, was filled with an optimistic belief in a 'civilisation machiniste' that was to find its prophet in Le Corbusier.

Giulio Carlo Argan examines this post-war situation as far as architecture, and particularly Gropius's work, were concerned, in his *Walter Gropius and the Bauhaus*: 'The two leaders in the renewal of European architecture were Le Corbusier and Gropius. Both fought for a rationalistic reform of architecture and their ideas had a good deal in common. But they were 'rationaliste' in opposite senses of the word, and each, faced with the same problem, found solutions to it that were quite contrary to the other's. Le Corbusier took rationalism as a system and made great plans to eliminate all problems; Gropius took it as a method that would allow him to discover and to solve the problems that life kept producing. The antithesis appears in their outward characteristics: Le Corbusier put out announcements and manifestoes, made propaganda trips around the world and shouted loudly: 'il existe un esprit nouveau'; Gropius shut himself up in his school, turned his theories into precise teaching practice and his logical ideas into techniques, and possibly wondered whether 'esprit' still existed. The historical situation underlines the contrast between them. Le Corbusier believed in a middle class that would be renewed by victory, and wished to help it to make peace after the war that had been a middle class war. He believed that the *civilisation machiniste,* which had, in fact, been one of the causes of the war, was a guarantee of future peaceful co-operation between peoples, and hoped to make every worker middle class, compensating for his loss of rights and the class struggle, by giving him a high standard of material wellbeing. The world was looking for new ethical ideas, and he offered it perfect social eugenics. By the time he realised that the *civilisation machiniste* was making cannon instead of houses, and began, in all good faith, to protest, the cannon were already knocking down the houses. Then he took refuge once again in immortal principles, became a 'pupil of nature', treated town planning like landscape gardening and dreamed of archaic, Mediterranean myths. In other words, he fell headlong from the future into prehistory . . . [whereas] Gropius, like Thomas Mann, belonged to the small group of intellectuals who faced what was happening in the German middle classes . . . yet did not despair of their eventual return to the old cultural traditions, believing that they would alter the aberrant way in which Germany was evolving and restore the authority of intelligence over a mad world.'

All this shows the outstanding importance of the Fagus Works. Both politically and artistically (if the distinction can still be made), it shows Gropius to be the leader of the school of modern European architecture. By 1911, Le Corbusier, who was four years younger than Gropius, was not yet working effectively; his plan for the Citrohan house, which tackled the problem of the mass-produced dwelling cell, belongs to the post-war period 1920–22. In the same year, 1911, Mondrian, who was born in 1872, was getting ready for his first trip to Paris, which was to bring him into contact with Cubism: it was a sort of incubation period before his support of the abstract, which came much later, around 1917. The only artist of the first half of the century who had already decisively cut his links with the past—and even with the present—that was still in process of moving ahead, as Cubism was, was Kandinsky, who in 1910, at the age of forty-five, had painted his first abstract watercolour, and had reached a position of mental freedom equal to that of Gropius, though very different in its application and in its methods.

Behrens's Turbine Factory may have influenced Gropius's plan for the Fagus Works, but, although geometrically it seems very new, the Turbine

3 Alfeld an der Leine.
Fagus Works, 1911.

Factory is really an example of the architectural monument, or of an aesthetic ideal which Behrens managed to dovetail with the function; although it came first, and the idea of the building's function followed after it. Behrens simplified his forms to their essential elements in a Cubist manner; in him, it is more a matter of style than an architectural use of the function – which is what it is in Gropius.

In the Fagus Works, Gropius's concept of space is completely new. He sees it not as something concrete, limited and defined by walls, and classified as interior or exterior space, through which the building appears an object, a closed geometrical figure; but as something created by the action of those who use it, and therefore a continuously regenerated, vital function of the man who works in it. This was the fundamental value of the Fagus Works at the start of Gropius's career: it was the living assertion of life's capacity to generate architecture as a 'way' or category of living itself, through a space that was not to be looked at, but to be used.

This theory, embodied in the Fagus Works, meant that a very large proportion of the building was of glass, for this was a material that could eliminate the surfaces of walls as they had so far been used – that is, with the object of limiting the space or making it seem objective. Argan writes: 'If we recall Alberti's distinction between the surface which belongs physically to things, and forms the noticeable skin in which they are confined in space, and the plane, as a pure section of projection of depth, it is easy to see that glass, as Gropius uses it, always has the function of a plane, never that of a surface.'

Of necessity, of course, the building has to be enclosed by a physical exterior, but instead of using the old surface to do so, this one uses the sectional plane, which eliminates at least part of the physical properties of a wall, because glass gives the eye the illusion of being immaterial. The lack of pillars at the corners, and thus the 'living' way in which the glass is joined at right-angles, means that continuous mouldings, which would make the planes appear as surfaces again, have to be eliminated; in the same way the narrow facing of the wall is set back in order to make the glass appear an airy space, and to avoid suggesting depth, which a direct confrontation with the concrete material of the wall could not fail to do.

The remarkable way in which the Fagus Works fits into a living situation seems to prevent any aesthetic judgements, as we tend to understand them, being made on it; indeed, its rigour, its strict rationalism, its declared intention of being made according to certain technical conditions, and in no way as a work of art or a monument, all prevent one from considering it so.

Indeed, the beauty and poetic significance of the Fagus Works are found in this: its refusal to become a work of art according to these standards, even though they may be extremely modern, which means that it is totally limpid and pure, and even today arouses a strong emotional reaction.

Reason appears to predominate throughout it: in the strong tension between steel and glass, or the interaction of vertical chimney and horizontal pipe, and in the way the space inside communicates with the reality outside, the two interpreting each other in a vital, regenerative way, yet leaving the perfect geometrical figure intact. The surrounding space, meanwhile, has been taken out of its historical context, yet, at the same time, the idea of the whole seems to come from a particular historical period, a vital one in the background of modern life.

**The Werkbund exhibition**

Between the Fagus Works and Gropius's second important work, the building for the Werkbund exhibition at Cologne in 1914, came a number of plans made mostly in collaboration with Adolf Meyer, who had already

worked on the Fagus Works and was to collaborate with Gropius on the Werkbund exhibition as well. These were:

A rail-car, for a factory making railway trucks at Königsberg. This was Gropius's first important attempt at industrial design, something he was later to pursue side by side with his architectural work, until he came to design the Adler car bodywork in 1929-30.

4–5 The Werkbund exhibition at Cologne, 1914. Office building: anterior façade and sideview, and interior façade.

Interior decoration for the World Fair at Ghent; awarded a gold medal.
Plan for a hospital at Alfeld an der Leine, with Meyer.
Plan for the regional councillor's office at Rummelsburg, with Meyer.
Plan for the Savings Bank at Dramburg, with Meyer.
Thirty single-family houses at Wittemberg (Frankfurt-on-Oder), with Meyer.
Plan for the Fitz district at Frankfurt-on-Oder, with Meyer.
Shops and regional plan for Poznań.
Dwelling houses for the workers at a car factory at Bernburg.
Warehouses at Märkisch Friedland.
Dwelling house at Semmering (Vienna).
The Kleffel cotton factory at Dramburg, with Meyer.
Furniture and interior decoration for Langerfeld, at Königsberg.

6 The Werkbund exhibition at
Cologne, 1914. Office building:
detail of one of the stair case
towers.

Furniture and interior decoration for Dr Hertzfeld, at Hanover.
Buildings for the von Brockhausen estate in Pomerania.

During the whole of the two years 1913–14, Gropius worked on the office building, with an exhibition gallery beside it, for the Werkbund exhibition.

Figs. 4–7

This was obviously a representative occasion, and so it did not really express his most deeply-held ideas; indeed, Argan has gone so far as to call it 'a display of architectural expressionism', and Leonardo Benevolo regards Gropius's part in it, not perhaps quite as a compromise, but at least as something of a departure from the admirable rigour of the Fagus Works. 'The delicate balance of the Fagus Works has changed,' he writes. 'The demands made upon Gropius are quite clear and his style shows all kinds of formal influences from Wright, from Behrens, from the Paris *Halle des Machines* of 1889, side by side, but not always successfully so.' This is the first time – which makes it important – that Wright's influence had been clearly seen in a European context.

The two parts, the main building and the exhibition hall, face each other:

Fig. 5
Fig. 4

deliberately, the more brilliant and modern façade of the main building is the one that faces the more truly industrial building, and the other façade, the outer one, which really represents the more public face of the group of

buildings, looks on to the street and has a merely representational object, with hints of the Werkbund's neo-romantic taste about it. Indeed, along the façade, up to the level of a clear-cut strip at the top, run slender pilasters, while the entrance is inserted, almost compressed, in the centre (with a function which appears to be merely monumental, something that would have been unthinkable in the Fagus Works). On either side of it are two cylindrical glass forms, projecting forward and enclosing the stairs; these side pieces are really a development of the back of the building, which is its pure centre, simply because it has no 'representational' function. Here, above a first row of small pilasters (whose rhythm is repeated by those on the back façade, and whose function is to detach and isolate the upper part) is a second portion of continuous glass, that uses the basic theme of the Fagus Works in an equally rigorous way. At either end two projecting glass façades go down to the ground and link up with the sides, developing into the small cylindrical towers mentioned earlier. This pure geometrical figure is completed by the central parallel pipes and two raised blocks holding the great flat roofs.

Fig. 6

All this would be merely a matter of stylistic success, however, if it were not linked with the exhibition gallery opposite it. This is a splendid example of geometrical purity, set beside the main block, in which the oblique lines of the roof are echoed in the clearly defined curve of the vertical walls.

Fig. 7

It might be called a translation of Behrens's monolithic, monumental Turbine Factory into a new period; but in this case it has a fluid relationship – an architectural one, but a social one as well – with the office building, which gives the whole a sense of structural unity.

Fig. 52

Wright's influence, which has been mentioned (and which is recognised by everyone who has studied Gropius's work) is clear in two ways: one, a matter of design and ideas, the other, a matter of style and technique.

First of all this means that the rejection of nature, which was also a rejection of all emotional involvement and which is typical of the Fagus Works, was modified. The Werkbund building has an open link with the reality around it, which is considered and valued as a natural one; the space, created by the action of the people using it, is seen in relation to an organic space that exists around it; these two kinds of space, the outer and the inner, interpenetrate each other in a way that is characteristic of Wright's work as well.

Thus Wright's influence is seen in the realm of ideas and design. In style and technique it is less important, or anyway, less successful and interesting. There is more emphasis upon the ornamentation of the walls, although they are not used, as they are in Wright's buildings, as a kind of natural material, humanised by the design and form, and upon the mouldings; and occasionally something that seems to be taken wholly from Wright appears–such as the entrance at the back.

It is important to consider this influence in Gropius's work. It would, indeed, seem to suggest that Gropius, with great moral courage, was admitting the insufficiency of the European tradition when it came to producing new architecture, and that therefore he was turning to something (the American tradition as it appeared in Wright), that in many ways was still, even historically, original and unexplored.

## The Bauhaus at Weimar

When the First World War broke out, Gropius was just over thirty; he was called up and saw active service until 1918, when he was demobilised. In the crisis, that followed it in Germany, he probably saw, with bitterness, his worst pre-war forebodings realised. Even before the war he had seen that all classes must take part in politics on a wider scale, that they must all become involved in the future of society. However, like his fellow intellectuals in Germany, he sought for civil and moral recovery in the very middle classes who had caused the war, and believed that they, the supposedly enlightened, could rebuild society. As far as Gropius was concerned, this meant through architecture; all that this reconstruction implied appeared later, in the remarkable ideas that emerged from his teaching at the Bauhaus.

A few months after he was demobilised in 1919, Gropius was put in charge of the Grossherzögliche Sächsiche Kunstgewerbeschule and of the Hochschule für bildende Kunst, at Weimar; and he made them into a single institute that took the name of *Staatliche Bauhaus*. His ten years as director, until 1928, were probably the most important decade for European art in this century, and in it the Bauhaus became a vital centre of ideas and plans, a professional and social force that influenced artistic production enormously, widening the frontiers of industry and actually creating industrial design. If one considers how profoundly our present way of life is conditioned, for good or ill, by the relationship between art and industry, by the possibility that artistic objects (a chair, a table, a car), may be very widely distributed, one realises the extent to which the work of Gropius and his school influenced history, for it was the Bauhaus that studied, put forward and launched the ideas that brought this about.

The teaching traditions of the Bauhaus went back to Ruskin and Morris. The rise of industry and its increasing power had meant that the artistic object, which was the legacy of craftsmanship, had been brutally produced on a large scale by industry, while the craftsman had failed to renew the spiritual meaning of the work of his hands. This had led to the decline of culture and thence to a decline in taste.

Besides this, there was another reason for the decline of craftsmanship, apart from the crushing effects of industry upon it. Craftsmanship had been defined as a 'minor art', a distinction being made between the artist, who creates 'major art', and the craftsman who makes objects for daily, material use (in other words, the object in everyday use). Gropius did away with the distinction between artist and craftsman: 'Complete construction is the final object of the visual arts . . . all of us, architects, sculptors, painters, must return to the crafts. Art is not a profession, there is no essential difference between the artist and the craftsman . . . We form a single community of craftsmen, without class distinctions . . . Together, we conceive and create the new building of the future, which will include architecture, sculpture, and painting in a single united form, and which one day will be raised to the skies by the hands of millions of workers.'

This attitude contained social as well as aesthetic ideas, and in the post-war urge for renewal, when, encouraged by the Russian Revolution, the working

class was struggling to make radical reforms in the bourgeois structure of economic life, Gropius's plan sounded like a call to unite ideas and work together, an idea that had prompted all his previous activity. Around this programme, Gropius collected many of the best European minds of his day: Itten, Feininger, Marcks and Meyer were his earliest associates; later Klee, Schlemmer, Kandinsky, Moholy-Nagy, Albers and Breuer came to teach at the Bauhaus; Albers and Breuer as pupil-teachers.

8 Berlin. Sommerfeld House, 1921.

The courses were three and a half years long. After an introductory course lasting one term, in which the student considered problems of form (the teaching was both theoretical and practical, and the students had their own workroom), he went on to a three-year course in one of the specialised workrooms. At the end of the course he received the diploma of Craftsman, and after a second, and stiffer, examination, the diploma of Craftsman of the Bauhaus. A course of further study followed, its length varying according to the student's abilities, which gave the title Master of Art, and later Master of Art of the Bauhaus.

The teaching plan was as follows:

PRELIMINARY SIX-MONTHS' COURSE
a. Teaching of the elementary theory of form
b. Study of materials in the workroom

TECHNICAL TEACHING FOR A THREE-YEAR COURSE
Sculpture (stone)
Cabinet-making (wood)
Metalwork (metal)
Ceramics (clay)
Mural painting (paint)
Weaving (fabrics)

WORKING EXERCISES
a. Materials and working tools
b. Elementary accountancy, study of prices, elements of contracts

FORMAL TEACHING FOR A THREE-YEAR COURSE, TOGETHER WITH TECHNICAL TEACHING
*Observation*
a. Study of nature
b. Analysis of materials

*Representation*
a. Descriptive geometry
b. Theory of building
c. Design and construction of plans

*Composition*
a. Theory of space
b. Theory of colour
c. Theory of composition

ARCHITECTURE

Too much has been written about the Bauhaus for us to deal with the subject in any detail here. Besides, although Gropius's influence on his school was extremely important, he was not the whole Bauhaus, nor was the Bauhaus the whole of him—nor of Klee, nor of Kandinsky, nor of Albers. So many teachers working closely together and with their students, and their productive relationship with industry, probably made the Bauhaus as similar to a large medieval artists' workshop (for instance, a cathedral workshop) as was possible in the modern world; yet individual personalities were not lost in the work of the group, as they were in a medieval workshop. The sense of individuality was too strong for that. From the time of the Renaissance this sense of individuality has been with us, and it was to combat it, or rather to combat its degeneration, that the Bauhaus was set up in the modern world; however, it was not able to cut out the historical marks it had made upon the whole personality of modern man.

Gropius's belief that there was no difference between artist and craftsman made him and his associates abolish all distinctions between teachers and students. Group work involved all forms of labour, and teaching was seen as a means of achieving the object of the exercise in a common effort to understand the reason for it and its spirit.

Another essentially important point was the school's relationship with industry. The teaching course was conceived as a gradual advance towards production, and so its final justification would come only from production itself; besides, the Bauhaus could not afford to function without making the best economic use of the work it produced. Many of the objects that have entered our daily life—furniture, books, advertisements, modern graphic designs—are derived from plans handed over to industry by the Bauhaus. Finally, the Bauhaus may be said to have built the perfect model or plan for a democratic society, Plato's Republic or St Augustine's *civitas dei,* in modern times; but its fatal flaw was that it was a model of the *élite,* a chosen, enlightened and progressive society that was drawn from above rather than pushed up from below. In other words, it was a very noble, fragile model of society, in a world shaken by fundamental struggles, the solution of which we have yet to see.

**From Sommerfeld House to the theatre at Jena**

The Bauhaus remained in Weimar until 1925, when the opposition of leading reactionary groups in the government of Thuringia forced it to move to Dessau. The most enlightened groups in Europe had identified it with the very spirit of modern art, but so had the most reactionary of the middle classes, to whom modern art meant revolution. Hypocritically, they called it 'Degenerate Art'—a good screen to hide behind—and decided it must be suppressed. A few years later the Bauhaus teachers were to see their work prominent in exhibitions officially labelled 'degenerate', organised by the Nazis.

Gropius's activity at Weimar began with the building of Sommerfeld Fig. 8 House (Berlin-Dahlem) in 1921. Signs of the Bauhaus idea can clearly be seen in this small wooden house, particularly in the renewed significance with which wood, a craftsman's material, is used in it. This use of wood has a

22

9 Project for a dwelling house, 1922.

10 Jena Municipal Theatre, 1922.

11 Project for the Academy of Philosophy at Erlangen, 1923.

12 Project for a house on the beach, 1924.

Fig. 4

historical point, a working tradition that in Gropius's case determined the elementary forms—beams, angles and masses. The relationship with Wright's Prairie Houses has been pointed out as well. Sommerfeld House does indeed seem to be an 'object' for dwelling in, something really basic to the ideas of the Bauhaus, planned so that the space—that is, its vital function—is linked to the quality of the materials, and the handwork in it is linked to the rational plan, ideas and execution being closely united. Probably Gropius felt at the time that the richest and most genuine source of ideas for this kind of attempt was Wright's Prairie Houses, which had grown from the pioneering spirit of America; in them, an architecture that sprang from traditions of craftsmanship produced a concept of life as intense as it was fruitful. Sommerfeld House develops and goes far beyond the links with Wright which were evident in the Werkbund building. There, Wright's influence was seen in the entrance, inserted, as it were, on the main façade; here the influence is properly developed to produce a façade whose horizontal lines are emphasised by jutting cornices, divided into three, so that the main door—with its contrast of masses and surfaces, light and shade—dominates. The choice of material, too, is another development of Wright's influence, a material which is successfully contrasted, in its own authenticity, with the triangular panes of glass in the windows.

In the following year, 1922, Gropius built his War Memorial at Weimar, again making the most of the material he used in relation to space and

24

13 View of the Bauhaus at Dessau as a whole, 1925–26.

movement. This time it was not wood–a material that suggests a whole history of craftsmanship behind it, to determine the kind of form the work will take–but cement, which Argan calls 'an artificial material, born of the form itself, without which it is nothing but a fluid, muddy mass.' Clearly this was a step forward in the process of integrating art and craft, which was one of the basic themes of the Bauhaus: man's history was enriched by the use of a new, untreated material, through a form that was born out of the possibilities of the material itself, and which was therefore a form of its own, absolutely authentic, in no way imitative.

A dwelling house Gropius built with Meyer, also in 1922, continues in the same direction. The building is L-shaped, but each of the blocks consists in its turn of a collection of cubic or prismatic blocks, undisturbed by any jutting cornices or roofs, in which the windows break the continuity of the walls by being cut deeply into it as into a mass of cement. Judging from the model, the building seems conceived like a great concrete sculpture, its two masses hinged, as it were, at the angle of the letter L which they form; as if this piece of sculpture were rotating on its axis, and centrifugal force were acting upon it, the large double windows are all pushed to the end of the longer arm of the L, while the six smaller ones are set in the shorter arm at varying levels.

Shortly afterwards came the transformation of the State Theatre at Jena (1923–24), Gropius's only plan for a theatre. Argan writes of it:

Fig. 9

Fig. 10

25

'The size, the design, the flexible fragility of it, the very tone of its colours, all show that these pale walls were born, through a slow process of change, from the glass walls of the Fagus Works and the Werkbund exhibition building.' Sommerfeld House, and Gropius's other work in 1922, were also necessary stages on the way to it; and the theme that connects all five buildings is the relationship between the vital function of the space and the surrounding walls determined by that space, and, linked to this, the material from which these surrounding walls are made, the material that turns something seen merely on paper, graphically, into an architectural reality. In the Fagus Works, Gropius had rid himself of surfaces, that is, of the idea that particular walls should enclose a particular space by using glass; gradually, he achieved the same result, in Sommerfeld House, and then in the 1922 plans (through the Weimar War Memorial), by using space itself as material in a block of wood or concrete. Finally, in the theatre at Jena, the material again became part of space through Gropius's remarkable use of light and rhythm in the walls. The Theatre at Jena is, with the Fagus Works and the Bauhaus at Dessau, probably Gropius's greatest achievement. In it his ideas are marvellously balanced, black and white, like light and darkness, being contrasted and intermingled, without a single jarring element, as the entrance in the Werkbund building. In the buildings so far examined, it has only once been necessary to use the term 'façade'; this was in the case of the Werkbund exhibition building, and it is not surprising that it should be so, for it was an official building with a representational function embodied, as it always is, in the façade. Significantly, this façade was the least successful part of the building and seems to have been imposed, to some extent, by the temporary necessities of the occasion. If Gropius's other early buildings are considered, however, it is clear that none of them, strictly speaking, has a façade; they are all conceived in a total or circular way, which finds itself expressed very precisely in the Fagus Works, at the very start of his career.

There is a danger, though, that one may consider this totality of vision in purely aesthetic terms, and thus fail to come to grips with the real problem. Totality (or circularity) of vision is a direct result to considering space as a vital function of the person who uses it. The man who lives in a building is, or according to Gropius, should be, the centre of its birth and development; the arrangement of the rooms should answer to the demands of life and living. And from this it follows quite clearly that no single part of the building should dominate the rest, for each part of living is equally necessary because equally real, which means that each part is of equal importance in the context of the whole. Obviously, if the building is conceived *from within*, it will have no façade; just as, when social and political pressures are stronger than architectural ideas, the façade is of primary importance. It is no coincidence that the age in which the façade of the building was at its most important and triumphant was that of the Counter Reformation, when the religious and civil powers imposed their authority through a powerful manifestation of awe-inspiring grandeur.

Gropius's plan for a dwelling house, made in 1922, thus takes on a less formal air: the 'rotary movement', which gives building its dimension in space, is really the visual translation of the vital function which actually determines the building. The two arms linked into an L-shape correspond to the fullness of vision transmitted from the interior to the exterior of the house, and there is a new, free relationship between the house and the land around it, a relationship that makes it part of a larger scheme.

This plan, from 1922, foreshadows the Bauhaus at Dessau more tellingly than any other. In 1923, Gropius planned the Academy of Philosophy at Erlangen, with Meyer. This time the L-shaped plan was more complex (there was a series of double L's, interlocking to make axes of rotation for

Fig. 11

14 View of the Bauhaus at Dessau as a whole, 1925–26.

15 The Bauhaus at Dessau, 1925–26. Detail of the bridge spanning the roadway, and the laboratories section.

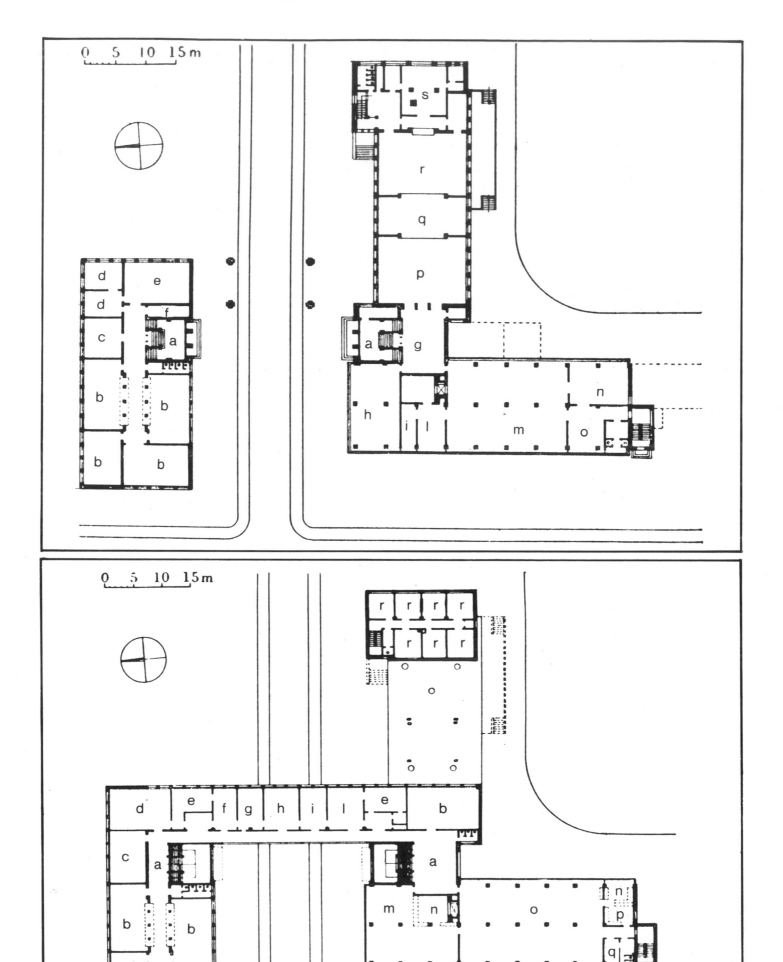

16 Opposite page, top: Ground-plan of ground floor of the Bauhaus. a) entrance b) classrooms c) cloak-room d) laboratories e) physics laboratory f) dark room g) entrance hall h) exhibition room i) model room 1) wash room m) carpentry shop n) machine room o) cabinet-making workshop p) auditorium q) stage r) dining-hall s) kitchen.

17 Opposite page, bottom: Ground-plan of first floor of the Bauhaus. a) entrance hall b) classrooms c) teachers' room d) library e) typists' room f) administration room g) reception hall h) management i) administration of the Bauhaus l) accounts room m) basic instruction room n) cloak-room o) weaving room p) instructors' room q) dressing-room r) studios.

18 The Bauhaus at Dessau, 1925–26. Detail of the laboratories section.

19 The Bauhaus at Dessau, 1925–26. Detail of the bridge spanning the roadway.

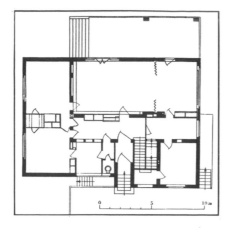

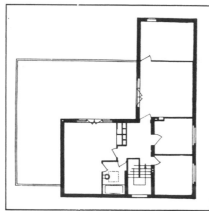

20–22 The Bauhaus at Dessau, 1925–26. The principal's house: East view and plan of the ground and first floors.

the whole building), but there is still the idea of a block linking the main blocks, and the idea of a relationship between horizontals and verticals, only briefly suggested in the previous year's plan, the verticals being used as hinges to pin the structure to the ground at points of stress, and the horizontals freeing themselves to make planes in space.

It is interesting to see how Gropius's ideas of planning appear not merely in the arrangement of large groups of buildings, like the Academy at Erlangen, which could create a whole new city around itself, but in small buildings as well. The very fine plan for the von Klitzing house on the beach, made in 1924, with its clean block with vertical lines and its horizontal verandah, is, just like the Academy, able to suggest the space around it; in other words, it can be seen as part of the ideal city that Gropius was developing. When the Bauhaus moved to Dessau, Gropius planned its headquarters. Perhaps this was the most remarkable chance he ever had of expressing, in a single group of buildings, his ideas on teaching, his social attitudes, and his thoughts as an architect. This, of course, explains its very high quality.

Figs. 14–27

There was only one possibility: Gropius planned a social microcosm that would be a model to humanity and was able to translate this into concrete terms, in a new form of planning (which was more than a new architecture). The following had to be included in the plan: technical school, workshops, administrative offices, recreational rooms, studies and living quarters for the students, and living quarters for the staff.

Gropius decentralised the three main functions: he put the technical school, the workshops, and the students' living quarters into three blocks, linking the technical school and the workshops by a bridge on which were the administrative offices, and the technical school and the students' living quarters by a single-storey arm in which were the recreational rooms (auditorium, theatre) and the dining room. This produced a structure made up of two L's which were joined to form a kind of swastika. The arrangement

Fig. 9
Fig. 11

was much more complex than it had been in the plan of '22 or the Academy of Philosophy at Erlangen – for instance, there was the bridge which included ways of communication between the buildings, as would happen in a town plan – but the basic idea was the same. In the 1922 plan, Gropius had already considered separating the two main blocks (one of which was made up of several different ones put together) and linking them by a short, single-storey arm. He had also used a plan unlike that of traditional town planning (streets with the fronts of the buildings lined up along them), to make a space in which every building could be seen from all points on

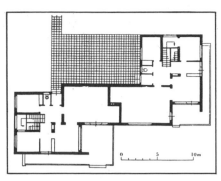

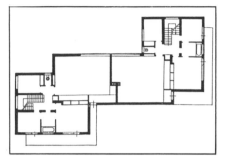

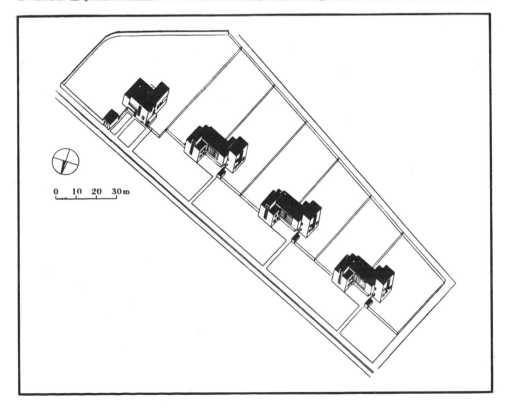

23–27 The Bauhaus at Dessau, 1925–26. Teachers' semi-detached houses: views and plans of the first floor; isometric drawing.

the horizon, and people in turn could look at all points on the horizon. This was, indeed, 'total' space.

But the group of Bauhaus buildings is planned in so exemplary a way, that it needs more careful examination; and this careful look will make clear the spirit of the society that occupied it.

The first L includes the workrooms, and through an entrance on the longest side, near the point of intersection with the second L, one enters the connecting arm, the students' living quarters and studies. The entrance opens into a hall that both connects and divides these and the connecting arm: on the right of the work-rooms is the exhibition hall, the staff room, the carpentry shop (the biggest room after it in the whole group of buildings is the weaving room on the first floor), the machine shop, and the wood-working room; on the left, in the connecting arm, the auditorium, the theatre, the dining room, and finally living quarters for the students and service rooms. On the first floor, there is a hall like the one on the ground floor; from this, one turns right into a practice room and then on into the enormous weaving workroom, which leads by a short passage to a store room and staff rooms, and then to the staircase at the head of the shorter arm of the L. On the left is a long gallery in which, after a classroom, are the administrative offices that occupy the longer arm of the second L: typists' rooms, accounts and administrative offices, reception rooms. The bridge building links these blocks to the technical school, which has four classrooms on the first floor, two workrooms, the physics laboratory, the dark room, and a store room; on the second floor there are another four classrooms, the library, and the teachers' room. Finally, the block containing the students' living quarters includes seven studies, above the living rooms, on the second floor.

It is easy to work all this out on the plan, and it is not a waste of time to do so; indeed, the very meaning of the Bauhaus can be found in the way the space is used, which means in the relationship of the vital functions to one another. Gropius's plan for a unity of teaching, education and art, craftsmanship and production, that is, the basic principle of the Bauhaus, can be seen even in the way the various parts of the building are divided into varying centres of activity (even living being an activity), and the way in which there is a continuous flow and movement between the various rooms and functions.

Figs. 20–27     Four small houses for the director and staff of the Bauhaus stand near this group of buildings, their arrangement again foreshadowing the way in which Gropius's town planning ideas were to develop in the future.

All Gropius's earlier plans and ideas, indeed, find themselves echoed and developed in the Bauhaus buildings. But what is really important is the

Fig. 9     totality of his vision, of his use of space, and the remarkable way in which

Fig. 11     he used the reality of life in this ideal city of his. It must not be forgotten

Fig. 12     that the Bauhaus was a social organism before it was an architectural one, a plan for a new kind of society that united all human functions: education and learning and production, thought and action, the work of the craftsman and the work of the artist, the activities of man and those of the machine. In other words it was 'the new building of the future, which would include architecture, sculpture and painting . . . raised to the sky by millions of workers.'

Between 1926 and 1928 Gropius made his first great town plan, the four rows of houses (the first and second in 1926, the third in 1927, the fourth in

Figs. 28–32     1928), in the Törten district of Dessau for the Reichsforschungsgesellschaft. These dwelling units were of four basic types, partially built from pre-fabricated elements, and they carry on Gropius's ideas on the theme, which he had incorporated in the four small houses at the Bauhaus, using a very simple structure and an unadorned style. However, his ideas of more general

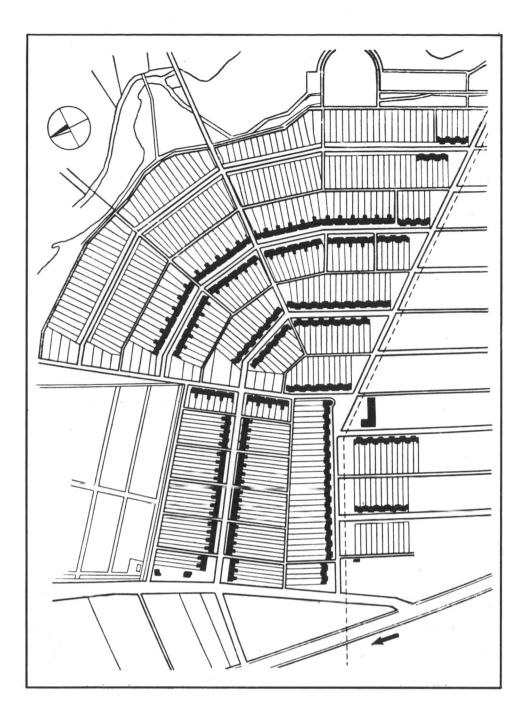

urban planning, found in the Bauhaus itself, are not as successfully applied on this larger scale.

Certainly, in looking at the general plan of the district, it is clear that, like that of the Bauhaus, it is totally used and handled. But it is equally true that this is an abstract opinion which can be arrived at only on paper, or by flying over the district; this means that it is lost – that is, *it does not exist* – for anyone actually living in the district, for whom the place as a whole should have a vital function.

The arrangement of the houses in rows radiating out from, or in concentric arcs around, the co-operative shop seems to link them into a well-arranged, enjoyable whole; yet the repetitive way in which they are related to one another makes streets seem like places in which a man is forced to walk, instead of making him feel – as he would at the Bauhaus – like an individual working in a whole to which he belongs in every way. It makes him feel like an isolated unit in a whole to which he belongs physically, more than anything; in other words, it perpetuates the traditional situation of man in society.

Obviously, one must not suggest that Gropius meant more than he said. The system he was using at Dessau-Törten was very different from the

Fig. 28

33

29 Houses of the kind built at Dessau-Törten, 1927.

30–32 Types of houses built at Dessau-Törten 1927 (left) and 1928 (right); plans of the ground and first floors.

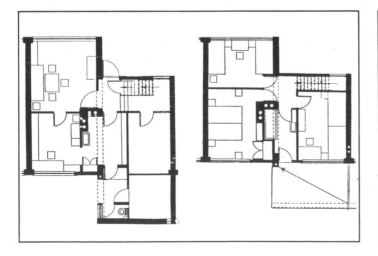

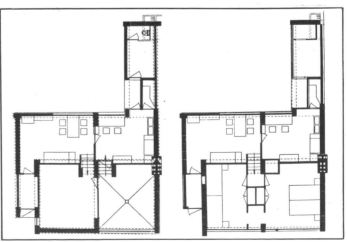

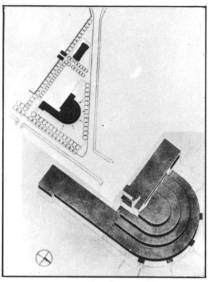

33–34 Labour office at Dessau. Detail of the interior and geometric plan.

social microcosm of the Bauhaus. In Germany in 1926, the Bauhaus community which produced the arrangement of the buildings was purely Utopian; as, indeed, it would still be today. And this was a fact of life that no architect could alter.

Gropius could, of course, have changed living conditions more radically by using the mass-produced building elements which were necessary in industry and so, according to Bauhaus principles, in aesthetics as well, while rejecting repetitiveness in his use of space; that is, he could have used something like the living space of the Bauhaus buildings instead of the unit of street, house and garden, which is, substantially, what Dessau-Törten uses; and this would have been a great revolution. But at this point it seems likely that Gropius, perhaps unconsciously, accepted as basic the social organisation in which he happened to be living, an organisation which the Bauhaus was challenging (but—as has already been said—it was the challenge of an *élite*). Indeed, the whole of Gropius's later work progressively drew nearer to what Argan, in speaking of Le Corbusier, called 'social eugenics', that is, a highly rational improvement of living conditions, not their overthrow in any really fundamental way.

Dessau-Törten, in a sense, ends Gropius's working cycle at the Bauhaus, not so much because he resigned from it in 1928 and went back to his professional work in Berlin, as because his later work shows that he had gone not necessarily beyond but away from his ideals and ideas in the previous decade.

The idea of architecture as town planning is not new; what is new is the way in which Gropius tackled it at the time. He found in society a collective structure and studied what its needs and its ideals might be. As Le Corbusier was to do later, and more completely, in his *villes radieuses*, he dealt with the relationships between individuals and society by transferring some of the tasks and activities traditionally kept within the family (recreational and educational, including those taking place at school) not to society as a whole, but to the social group which was identified with the house, no longer envisaged as belonging to a single family.

This was a typically rationalistic formula, which foresaw the perfect equality of individuals and therefore the possibility of their combining in

35 Karlsruhe, Dammerstock
district, 1929–30. Detail of a
building.

36 Opposite page. Karlsruhe,
Dammerstock district, 1929–30.
Detail of a building.

37 Project for the Totaltheater,
1927. Isometric drawing.

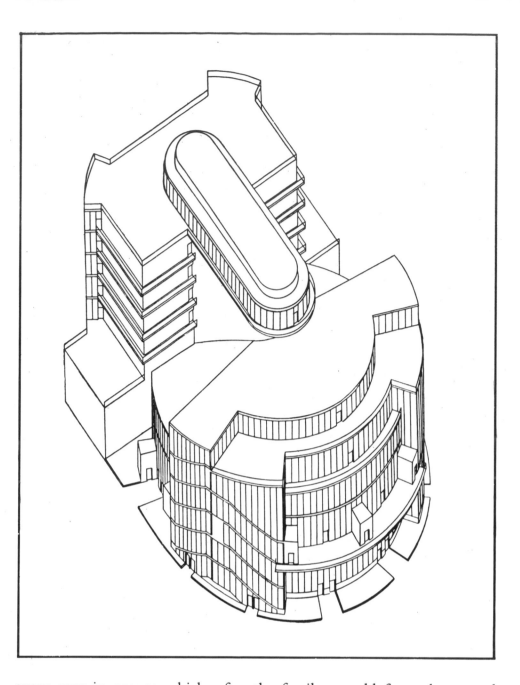

every way in groups which, after the family, would form the second
organisational layer of society. It was also a formula that had a touch of
class feeling about it: the conclusion is inescapably, that the possibility of
these groups being formed (which justifies building houses that have the
conditions necessary for them) really rests upon the fact that the members
of them all belong to the same social class. Indeed, the two great town

Pls. 5–12 Figs. 35, 36
Pls. 13–15
plans, for the Dammerstock district in Karlsruhe and the Siemensstadt in
Berlin (1929–1930), solved the problem of 'minimum living standards'
*(Existenz-Minimum)*, that is, they gave rational, comfortable homes to
the working classes, but in no way integrated these classes, from the town-
planning point of view, in the larger framework of the city.

Figs. 28–32
Within these limitations, however, both the Dammerstock and the
Siemensstadt districts are perfect. Unlike the houses at Dessau-Törten,
theirs are arranged in rows like the teeth of a comb, that is, perpendicular
to the roads, so that they repeat a constant relationship between full and
empty spaces, between living blocks and the surrounding space. Once
again, nature is denied all emotional value; or rather, what is denied is the
very existence of nature as it has been seen by a long romantic tradition,
and trees and flowerbeds, sky and horizon, are conceived as necessary
elements of a rational way of living, and as such distributed in exactly
equal parts for everyone to enjoy.

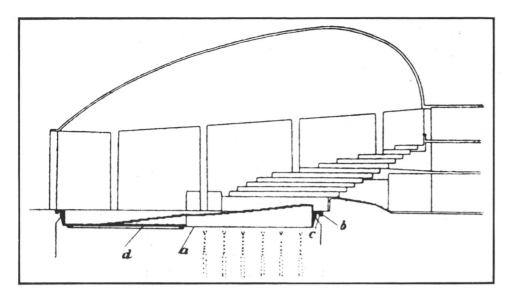

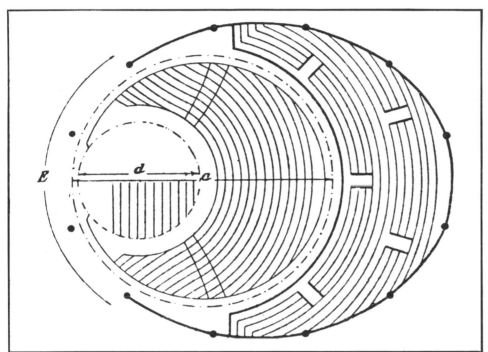

It is obvious that Gropius's mental structure, his education, and his previous experience prevented him from thinking of man as a bundle of emotions, rather than as a rational plan, and that is why Wright's influence upon his work is really so slight – certainly it in no way determines it (just as ideas of organic architecture did not alter it during his many years in America). However, in the work he did between the Fagus Works and the Bauhaus buildings in Dessau, there was a vital tension which filled them with something that can only be called humanity, an effort to encompass complete activity as the supreme purpose of life, which warmed his rigorous rationalism.

At this point, with the slackening of these interests, or perhaps because they were transferred to the much larger scale of total town planning, in which Gropius could not really breathe, the extremely high quality he had maintained for nearly twenty years as architect, teacher and inspirer slowly declined, and he became, more and more, a correct designer of good, rational dwellings.

At the same time he worked on other projects which can all be considered part of his idea of town planning, since they were used for the functions which modern society expects the community to deal with: themes like the distribution of labour and education.

It concerned a number of buildings, either built or not, such as the plan

Figs. 37–39

Figs. 33, 34

Fig. 41
Fig. 42

for the Totaltheater for Piscator (1927), the Labour Office in Dessau (1927–28), the Co-operative store in Dessau-Törten (1928), the Engineering School at Hagen (1929), the plan for a theatre at Charkov (1930), and the plan submitted for the competition for the Soviet Headquarters in Moscow (1931).

All these undoubtedly form part of his ideas on town planning, but as they are not made at the same time, they overcome the limitations – even limitations of quality – which Gropius had as a town planner. In recent years the difficult tests which mass architecture requires the architect to undergo have not been satisfactorily passed in the case of the dwelling-house (Le Corbusier's plan for Dom-Ino, in 1914, had already forecast this); but in the buildings in which modern society best expresses itself, such as stations, stadiums, theatres, schools, hospitals, and so on, and in some cases even churches (if we think of Ronchamp), the very highest levels have been reached. Gropius was no exception, and during his last years in Germany – he left for England in 1934, in opposition to the Nazis – his best work was found not in the town plans already mentioned, or in others, like the experimental district of Spandau-Haselhorst, which he submitted for a competition in 1929, and for which he won a prize, but in public buildings. These public buildings, it must be emphasised, have nevertheless a function in town planning. Their social function is related to the masses, they deal with urban spaces, and they are linked with the ideal collectivist city which was ever in Gropius's mind.

Figs. 37–39

When he designed his Totaltheater for the actor Piscator, all the technical and architectural arrangements were derived from Gropius's initial conviction that modern society must entrust new tasks and new possibilities to the theatre. It was no longer a mere sideshow to distract the lower classes from responsible activity, still less was it for the kind of performance which an eighteenth-century *élite* had envisaged when it built its theatres in hierarchical terms (stalls, circle, boxes). On the contrary, the theatre must revive sensibility, it must be an active spiritual force, with which man, worn by industrial labour, recharged his own vital processes; in the end, it was a much-needed school for the mind. In other words, it was a theatre

40 Villa at Zellendorf, 1928.

41 Project for the theatre at Charkov, 1930. Plan.

42 Project for the Soviet Headquarters in Moscow, 1931.

for all, taking its form from all the interests at the centre of which it stood, and thus becoming a *complete* theatre.

The Totaltheater not only rejected any hierarchical seating of the audience, it abolished the division between stage and stalls: the action on the stage must be entirely participated in by the audience, not imposed upon it.

The theatre's plan envisaged two rotary movements, one on the circular stage (or rather semi-circular, if the space is really total), turning on itself, the other in part of the auditorium, which was also circular and included the stage itself. When this second movement was made, the stage was no longer at the apex of the elipse that formed the plan of the theatre, but almost in the centre of it, recreating the old form of the amphitheatre. Gropius himself said that it was 'born from the tragic arena, in which the performance developed on the whole spherical front at once, the actor being the voice of the whole audience placed concentrically around him.'

This may sound as if everything takes place on one level. In fact, this is not so, and the movement is not just horizontal. The proscenium can be raised or lowered, the lighting involves the entire space, which is made concrete, architecturally, in the form of an egg.

Curved forms also appear in the Labour Office in Dessau (1927–28), another typically social, urban plan, in which Gropius used continuous semi-circular lines, making a sort of magnet which was to draw to it, in an almost symbolic way, the moving flow of the city's labour, which it mixed and organised.

A little earlier, in 1931, he entered for the competition for the Soviet Headquarters in Moscow. In this, the radial structure may have symbolised the fact that everyone had a hand in public affairs and could take part in them in a new world. Russia must indeed have seemed a new world to an enlightened German, at a time when Germany itself was diving into the most terrible, tragic circumstances; but it may be interpreted in the opposite way–as a symbol of the concentration of power, a metaphor for iron rule.

These works, and later ones at exhibitions between 1931 and 1934 (a hall at the Paris Exhibition, the Exhibition of non-ferrous materials in Berlin, etc.), brought Gropius's work in Germany to an end. In England and in America his work was to be of value more from the teaching than from the architectural point of view; it was to seek to bring the world of architecture up to date, rather than to bring anything new and creative to it.

The three years Gropius spent in England, from 1934 to 1937, during which he worked in collaboration with Maxwell Fry, must in retrospect probably be considered a happy interval before final departure for America. Town planning was not a part of his work: in England he built only a few houses, the school at Impington and other schools (the school for the Sanatorium at Papworth, the school at Histon), and working premises for London Film Productions. All this followed what he had been doing on similar buildings built or planned in Germany; for instance, the villa at Zellendorf in 1928, which developed an idea he had already touched upon in the four small staff houses of the Bauhaus at Dessau.

Argan has remarked that for Gropius his stay in England and then in America was a kind of homecoming: 'From England, the first stage of his exile, had come the first message of the social function of art, with Ruskin and Morris; from England had come the spirit of practical work, which Germany had long forgotten, and the first impulse of its great industrial progress . . . As for America, one need only recall that Morris had given American realism the religious leaven that made the architecture of Sullivan and Wright the expression, and almost the symbol, of the most genuine, Lincoln-like democracy. For Gropius, it was like going back to the origins of his own ideological tradition, finding once more his faith in the 'progress' which, in Europe, after its first exuberant flowering, had been all too quickly

Figs. 56–58

Figs. 43–45

Fig. 40
Figs. 20–27

43 Opposite page, top. Ben Levy's house in Chelsea, London, 1936.

44–45 Opposite page, centre and bottom. Impington School, 1936.

46–49 Cambridge (Massachusetts). Harvard University. Project for the Graduate Centre, 1948.

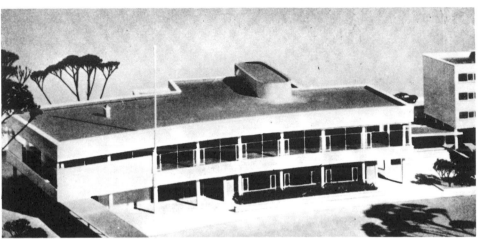

50 Opposite page. Berlin. Building in the Britz-Buckow-Rudow district (Gropiusstadt), 1964–68.

corrupted by the aggressive selfishness of the ruling classes.'

On the other hand, the rapid decline and exhaustion of German social democracy, and the disappearance of a world in which its fragile ideals were betrayed by the ferocity of the Nazi and Fascist dictatorships, meant that the perfect Utopian plans of rationalism, of which that world had sought to be the image and the manifesto, were lost as well; not merely through external political events, but through its own incapacity to find a real solution to the evils of society. Gropius's plans for Dessau-Törten, Dammerstock and Siemensstadt are the final act of a Utopia that avoids concrete reality and replaces it with plans that can be repeated an infinite number of times.

Figs. 28–32
Pls. 5–15 Figs. 35, 36

In America Gropius courageously compared what he had learnt in Europe with the new reality before him, and equally bravely gave up his earlier rationalism in favour of architecture and planning, that were more open to the endless mobility of American life. However, his work in the last decades of his life is important more on the theoretical and didactic plane, than on the level of actual building. Once he had broken away from rationalism, he was left, in America, with the clear terms of a style he had earlier used with far greater moral strength (the strength of a reformer seeking a new society, not that of a technician–as he now was–who gave the best image of a society he had accepted). He remained a subtle artist, a remarkable visual technician, but no longer a revolutionary, who, like Marcel Breuer, had grown up with the Bauhaus; he had left the plans of a long life of the spirit and of intellectual effort, which could be used in any number of variations. He worked and taught at a very high level: TAC (The Architects Collaborative), which he founded in 1945 with a group of his pupils, is probably the most authentic expression of his final period. This was a period of correct, beautiful and indeed, very fine plans which, nevertheless, lack the intellectual quality, the polemical tension, and the rigorous faith of his younger years–the years of rationalism and reform, which may have failed, yet are eternal.

Pls. 17–40 Figs. 46–50

1

2-3

4

5

10

12

14-15

16

18-19

24

25

34

40

# Description of colour plates

## Biographical outline

Walter Gropius was born in Berlin in 1883, into an old family originally from Braunschweig. From 1903 he studied architecture in the universities of Berlin and Munich, although he did not take a degree, and visited Spain, Italy, France, England and Denmark.

Back in Germany, in 1907, he went to work in the office of Peter Behrens, one of the leading figures of the new European architecture, and became chief assistant until 1910, when he set up his own professional office in Berlin. From 1910–11 he worked on plans for the Fagus Works, a shoe-factory at Alfeld.

Until the outbreak of war in 1914 he worked intensely as architect, planner and designer, and his interior decoration for the World Fair at Ghent won the gold medal in 1913.

Throughout the war he saw active service, and after his demobilisation in 1918 he took over the direction of the Grossherzögliche Sächsische Kunstgewerbeschule and the Hochschule für bildende Kunst, at Weimar. The two were fused into the Bauhaus (Staatliche Bauhaus), with Gropius as principal until 1928. In 1925 it was transferred from Weimar to Dessau, after opposition from the government of Thuringia under pressure from reactionary groups. Many of the major European artists worked at the Bauhaus: Herbert Bayer, Marcel Breuer, Josef Albers, Lászlò Moholy-Nagy, Wassily Kandinsky, Paul Klee, Lyonel Feininger, Johannes Itten, Gerhard Marcks, Adolf Meyer, Georg Muche, and Oskar Schlemmer.

During his time at the Bauhaus, Gropius, besides teaching, continued his architectural work, and it was in those years that he produced the work which

is universally considered his masterpiece, the group of buildings to house the Bauhaus at Dessau (1926).

In 1928, Gropius handed over the direction of the Bauhaus to Hannes Meyer, and took up his professional work in Berlin. In the same year he was involved in the founding of C.I.A.M. (Congrès Internationaux d'Architecture Moderne), and was nominated vice-president.

From then onwards he concerned himself most of all with problems of town planning, and his most important work is the Siemensstadt district in Berlin (1929).

After the Nazis seized power, he fled to England, in 1934, where he designed dwelling houses and schools, in collaboration with Maxwell Fry, and exercised a profound influence upon English architecture.

In 1937 he left England for the United States. He had been offered the Chair of Architecture at the Graduate School of Design at Harvard, and in 1938 he was made President of it, a position he held until 1951. His teaching and his professional work were still informed by the principles of the Bauhaus; he collaborated with Marcel Breuer and Wachsmann, with whom he promoted a system of prefabrication for dwelling houses.

In 1945 he became associated with a group of young architects, among them a number of his pupils, and produced TAC (The Architects Collaborative). TAC brought out a large number of plans, one of the most important of which is probably that of the Graduate Centre for Harvard University, built in 1950.

The final period of Gropius's life was still intensely busy: the Interbau building in Berlin, the United States Embassy in Athens, the Boston Center, the University of Baghdad, the Britz-Buckow-Rudow headquarters in West Berlin.

He died in July 1969, still fully creative, at the age of 86.

51 Opposite page, top.
Walter Gropius in his school.

52 Opposite page, bottom.
Peter Behrens's Turbine Factory in Berlin.

53 Project for a prefabricated house for the General Panel Corporation, 1947 (with K. Wachsmann).

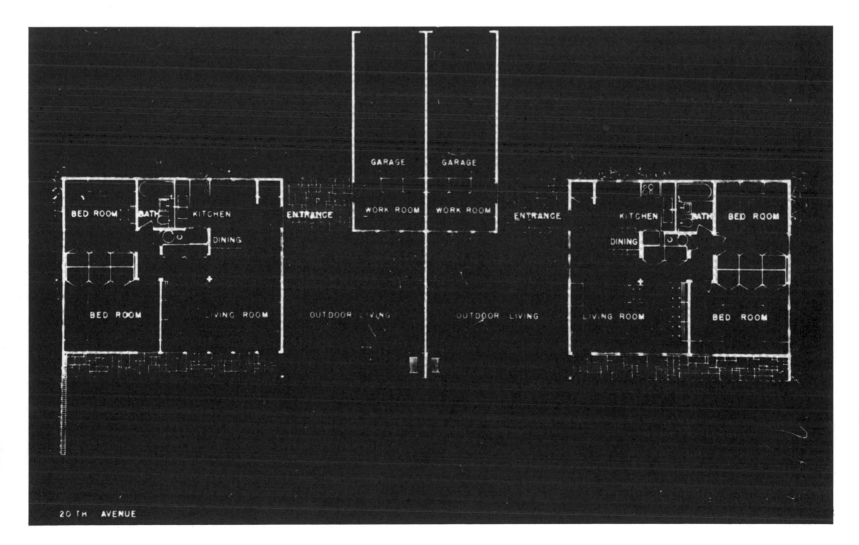

# Bibliography

## List of Gropius's main works

The list that follows has been compiled from the following works: G. C. Argan, *Walter Gropius and the Bauhaus,* Turin, 1951; S. Giedion, *Walter Gropius, The Man and his Work,* Milan, 1954; *Universal Encyclopedia of Art* (entry on Gropius by Ernesto N. Rogers', Rome, 1958; *Encyclopaedic Dictionary of Architecture and Town Planning* (entry on Gropius by Elio Piroddi), Rome, 1969.

**1906–1909**
Farm-workers' houses at Janikow near Dramburg, in Pomerania.

**1910–1911**
Fagus Works, shoe factory at Alfeld an der Leine, with A. Meyer (first building; the second was built in 1924–1925).

**1913–1914**
Rail-car for a factory making railway carriages at Königsberg. Interior decoration for the World Fair at Ghent (gold medal).
District of single-family houses at Wittemberg, Frankfurt-on-Oder, with A. Meyer.
Plan for the Fitz district of Frankfurt-on-Oder, with A. Meyer.
Plan for a hospital at Alfeld, with A. Meyer.
Plan for the regional councillor's office at Rummelsburg.
Plan for the Savings Bank at Dramburg, with A. Meyer.
Shops and regional plan for Posen (Poznań).
Dwelling house at Semmering (Vienna).
Dwelling houses for a car factory at Bernburg.
Shops at Märkisch Friedland.
The Kleffel cotton factory at Dramburg, with A. Meyer.
Furniture and decoration for Mendel, Berlin.
Furniture and decoration for Langerfeld, at Königsberg.
Furniture and decoration for Dr Hertzfeld, at Hanover.
Rural houses on the von Brockhausen estate in Pomerania.

**1914**
Office building and exhibition hall at the Werkbund exhibition in Cologne, with A. Meyer.
Pavilion for Deutz Engines, with A. Meyer. Steel furniture for the warship *Von Hindenburg,* with A. Meyer. Sleeping cars for the Reichsbahn. Bodywork for cars. Gerson furniture. (All these were on show at the Werkbund.)
Farm-workers' houses and shops at Dramburg.

**1921**
Sommerfeld house at Berlin-Dahlem.
Workers' houses for the Hess stocking factory at Erfurt (the plan, in which Gropius collaborated with A. Meyer, won second prize in the competition).
Plan for the *Chicago Tribune* skyscraper, with A. Meyer.

**1922**
Handle set in nickel.
War Memorial at Weimar
Building for the Bauhaus at Weimar.

**1923**
Plan for the Villa Hausmann at Pyrmont, with A. Meyer.

**1923–1924**
Transformation of the State Theatre at Jena.

**1924**
Auerbach House at Jena, with A. Meyer.
Plan for the Academy of Philosophy at Erlangen, with A. Meyer.
Plan for the Friedrich Fröbel Institute at Bad Liebenstein in Thuringia, with A. Meyer.
Hanover papermill at Alfeld, with A. Meyer.
Plan for the von Klitzing house on the beach, with A. Meyer.
Plan for the Engelhard workshops, with A. Meyer.
Entry for a competition for a plan for a banqueting hall at Frankfurt-on-Maine, with A. Meyer.
Reis and Mendel tombs in Berlin.

**1924–1925**
The Kappe shops at Alfeld, with A. Meyer.
Building annexed to the Fagus Works, with A. Meyer.

**1925**
Plan for the Benscheidt house at Alfeld an der Leine.
Reconstruction of the Benscheidt Jr. house at Alfeld an der Leine.
Plan for an old peoples' home at Alfeld an der Leine.
Plan for headquarters of the Teachers' Association at Dresden.
Plan for a sanatorium in Thuringia.
Exhibition of the Union of Mirrorworkers at Leipzig.
Gropius's own house and Bauhaus teachers' houses at Dessau.

**1925–1926**
The Bauhaus at Dessau.

**1926**
Müller factory at Kirchbraach.
First and second group of terrace houses at Dessau-Törten.

**1927**
Third group of terrace houses at Dessau-Törten.
Two prefabricated dwelling houses at the Werkbund exhibition at Stuttgart.
Plan for a co-operative store at Dresden.
Dairy at Törten.
Plan for a block of flats at Marburg.
Plan for the Hecke house at Hamburg.

Plan for small houses for the firm Molling and Co.
Plan for a house at the Ausstellung Press in Cologne.
Plan for the Totaltheater for Piscator.
The Zuckerkandl house at Jena.
Plan for wooden weekend houses.
Plan submitted for the competition for the Civic Centre at Halle (town hall, museum and sports grounds).
Plan for the Biesenhorst district in Berlin.

1927–1928
Municipal Labour Office in Dessau.
Dammerstock district at Karlsruhe (first prize in the competition).

1928
The Lewin house in Berlin-Zehlendorf.
Plan for the Harnischmacher house at Wiesbaden.
Plan for the country district at Dessau-Wolfen.
Plan for a co-operative district at Merseburg.
Co-operative store at Dessau-Törten.
Fourth group of terrace houses at Dessau-Törten.
Participation in the *Wohnen im Grünen* exhibition in Berlin.
Prefabricated copper houses for the Mirsch copper and brass factory at Finow.

Plan for apartment houses at Nagel-Nuremberg.
Kass interior decoration at Berlin-Zehlendorf.
Plan for apartment houses in Paris.

1931–1933
Stoves for the Frank factory.

1932
Plan for the reconstruction of the Adler workshops at Frankfurt-on-Maine.
Participation in the German exhibition 'The Extendable House'.
Plan for a club in Buenos Aires.
Plan for standardised houses in Buenos Aires.

1933
Plan for prefabricated houses at the A. Rosa Works in Barcelona.
Plan for the Reichsbank in Berlin, with J. Schmidt.
The Bahner house in Berlin.
The Maurer house in Berlin-Dahlem.

1934
Participation in the exhibition 'German People, German Work', with J. Schmidt.
Participation in the Exhibition of Non-ferrous Metals, in Berlin, with J. Schmidt.

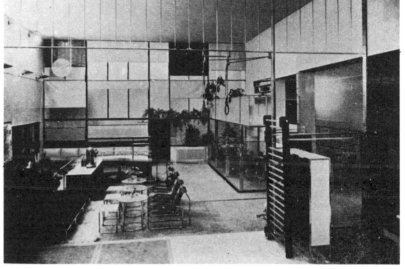

1929
Plan for the experimental district of Spandau-Haselhorst, Berlin (first prize in the competition).
Prefabricated furniture for the Feder shops in Berlin.
Plan for dwelling houses in Sommerfeld, Berlin.
Plan for a professional school in Berlin-Köpenick.
Plan for the Engineering School at Hagen, Westphalia (second prize in the competition).
Plan for an old peoples' home at Kassel.
Gagfah district at Lindenbaum, in Frankfurt-on-Maine.

1929–1930
Bodywork for Adler cars.
Siemensstadt district in Berlin, in collaboration with Bartning, Forbat, Häring and Sharon.
Research on the building of four-storey cheap houses and flats for the Reichsforschungsgesellschaft.

1930
Exhibition of the German Werkbund in Paris (theme: the community spirit in the tall house), in collaboration with Bayer, Breuer and Moholy-Nagy.
Plan for a house with steel structure.
Plan for the Law Courts in Berlin.
Plan for the theatre at Charkov (eighth prize in the International Competition).
Plan for houses of recreation and education at the Tiergarten in Berlin, with R. Hillebrecht.
Plan for a school of physical education in Schwarzerden.

1931
Participation in the German Architectural Exhibition in Berlin, with a meeting room and gymnasium.
Plan for the Erich Mendelsohn sanatorium.
Bienert tomb in Dresden.
Participation in the competition for a plan for the Soviet Headquarters in Moscow.
Electrical machinery for the Voss factory in Hanover.
Plan for houses with flats and equipment in common, on the Wansee in Berlin.

54 Opposite page. Project for the Chicago Tribune skyscraper, 1921.

55 Top. Adler car bodywork, 1929–30.

56 Top right. General hall at the Paris Exhibition, 1930.

57 Above. Tall house at the Berlin Exhibition, 1931.

93

**1935**
Plan for apartment houses at St Leonard's Hill, Windsor, with Maxwell Fry.
Ben Levi's house in London, with Maxwell Fry.

**1936**
Workshops for London Film Productions at Denham, with Maxwell Fry.
The Donaldson house in Sussex, with Maxwell Fry.
School at Impington Village, Cambridgeshire, with Maxwell Fry.
Plan for the school for Papworth Sanatorium, Cambridgeshire, with Maxwell Fry.
School at Histon, Cambridgeshire, with Maxwell Fry.
Plans for bedrooms at Christ's College, Cambridge.

**1937**
Plan for a kindergarten in Cambridge, Massachusetts.
Plan for the artistic centre at Wheaton College in Wheaton, Massachusetts, with Marcel Breuer (second prize in the competition).

**1938**
Gropius's own house in Lincoln, Massachusetts, with M. Breuer.
Breuer's house at Lincoln, Massachusetts, with M. Breuer.
House for Professor J. Ford in Lincoln, Massachusetts, with M. Breuer.
The Hagerty house in Cohasset, Massachusetts, with M. Breuer.

**1939**
The Chamberlain house in Sudbury, Massachusetts, with M. Breuer.
The Frank house in Pittsburgh, with M. Breuer.
State of Pennsylvania pavilion at the World Fair in New York, with M. Breuer.
The G. House at Lincoln, Massachusetts, with M. Breuer.
Plan for Black Mountain College at Lake Eden, North Carolina, with M. Breuer.

**1940**
Plan for a leisure centre at Key West, Florida, with K. Wachsmann.

**1941**
District of working-class buildings at New Kensington, near Pittsburgh (250 dwelling units and a common building), with M. Breuer.
House for Doctor Abele at Framingham, Massachusetts, with M. Breuer.

**1942**
Storrow Land Division at Lincoln, Massachusetts, with M. Breuer.
Plan for a convalescent home at Key West, Florida, with K. Wachsmann.

**1943–1945**
'Packaged House System', study of prefabricated houses for the General Panel Corporation, with K. Wachsmann.

**1944**
Jeweller's shop in New York.
Factory in Greensboro, North Carolina.
Factory in Cali, Colombia.

**1944–1948**
Architectural consultancy for the Container Corporation of America.

**1945**
Catholic church in Torreon, Mexico, with J. Gonzales Rejna.
From 1946, the year of the foundation of TAC, Gropius's work was planned in collaboration with TAC. Listed here are those buildings for which Gropius was directly responsible: see *Encyclopaedic Dictionary of Architecture and Town Planning,* (Dizionario Enciclopedico di Architettura e Urbanistica) mentioned earlier and in Bibliography.

**1946**
Town planning consultancy for Black Mountain College, with M. Breuer.
The Ryan house in Cambridge, Massachusetts–TAC.
The Poppleton house Dayton, Ohio–TAC.
Plan for the Lexington Nursery School in Lexington, Massachusetts–TAC.
Plan for a skiing hut in Franconia, New Hampshire–TAC.
Plan for the Library in Willimantic, Connecticut–TAC.
The Kaplan house in Newton, Massachusetts–TAC.
Plan for the Usiskin house in Long Island, New York.

**1947**
The Brockemann house in Worcester, Massachusetts–TAC.
The Neill house in Andover, Massachusetts–TAC.
The Wolfers house in Maine–TAC.
The Peter house in Cape Cod, Massachusetts–TAC.
The Catheron house in Foxboro, Massachusetts–TAC.
Reconstruction of the Heywood house in Maine–TAC.
Town plan for Michael Reese Hospital in Chicago.

**1948**
Plan for the Hua Tung University in Shanghai–TAC.
High School in Attleboro, Massachusetts–TAC.
The Lawrence house in Lexington, Massachusetts–TAC.
The McMahon house in Lexington, Massachusetts–TAC.
Dwelling house in Providence, Rhode Island–TAC.
The England house in Pittsfield, Massachusetts–TAC.
The Howlett house in Belmont, Massachusetts–TAC.
Plan for the primary school in Sherborn, Massachusetts–TAC.

**1948–1952**
Plan for the Wasco Flashing Corporation in Cambridge, Massachusetts–TAC.

**1949**
The Pillsbury house in Rumford, Rhode Island–TAC.
The Field house in Cape Cod, Massachusetts–TAC.

1949-1950
Graduate Centre for Harvard University in Cambridge, Massachusetts, with
TAC and Brown, Lawford and Forbes.

1950
Park buildings in Lexington, Massachusetts–TAC.
The Apthop house in Concord, Massachusetts–TAC.
The Hechinger house in Washington–TAC.
The England House in Washington–TAC.
The Napoli house in Concord, Massachusetts–TAC.
Plan for the Theatre in New Rochelle, New York–TAC.
Plan for the Medical Centre in Mount Kisco, New York–TAC.
Plan for the reconstruction of the Barnes house in Belmont, Massachusetts–TAC.

1951
Business school at Attleboro, Massachusetts–TAC.
Burneoat Secondary School and Senior School with thirty classrooms in
Worcester, Massachusetts, with TAC and A. Johnson.
Primary school with fourteen classrooms in Worcester, Massachusetts with TAC
and A. Roy.

The Pillsbury house in Milton, Massachusetts–TAC.
Furniture for the Vischer house in West Indiana–TAC.
The Vannah house in Foxboro, Massachusetts–TAC.
The Stichweh house in Hanover, Massachusetts–TAC.
Plan for primary school and secondary school in Amesbury, Massachusetts–
TAC.
Plan for the reconstruction of the Donelly Bureau in Boston–TAC.
Plan for the Bradley house–TAC.
Plan for quarters for the Technical Administration and Housing and Home
Finance Agency at San José de Costa Rica–TAC.

1951-1952
Thirty dwelling houses at Five Fields, Lexington, Massachusetts–TAC.
Three dwelling houses at Lake Barcroft, Falls Church–TAC.

1952
Plan for an office building for the American University in Washington–TAC.
West Side primary school with twenty classrooms in Taunton, Massachusetts–
TAC.
Two primary schools in Warwick and Providence, Rhode Island, the latter with
Harkness and Geddes–TAC.
Senior school with 32 classrooms in Concord, New Hampshire–TAC.
Office building for the American Association for Advancement in Science, in
Washington–TAC.
Shops for the Hechinger Company at Falls Church and Alexandria–TAC.
Designs and models for school and college furniture for the Thonet factory–
TAC.
The Cole house in Cambridge, Massachusetts–TAC.
The Baruch house in Newton, Massachusetts–TAC.
The Lang house in Newton, Massachusetts–TAC.
Primary school in Cambridge, Massachusetts, with TAC and C. Koch.
Primary school with 32 classrooms in North Adams, Massachusetts–TAC.
Reconstruction of the Caulfield house in Washington–TAC.

1953
Office building for McCormick and Company Inc. in Chicago–TAC.
Wherry district, with 35 dwelling units, for the Navy in Quonset, Rhode Island–
TAC.
Boston Back Bay Center in Boston, with TAC and P. Belluschi, H. Stubbins,
C. Koch and W. Bogner.
Plan for the National Education Association building–TAC.

1954
Flagg Street primary school in Worcester, Massachusetts, with TAC and A. Roy.
Shopping centre in Saugus, Massachusetts, with TAC and Ketchum, Gind,
Sharp.
Thoracic Clinic in Boston, Massachusetts–TAC.

1955
Primary school in Waltham, Massachusetts–TAC.
Secondary school in South Attleboro, Massachusetts–TAC.

1956
Primary school in West Bridgewater, Massachusetts–TAC.
Defence Housing, Otis Air Force Base in Falmouth, Massachusetts–TAC.
Block of flats in the Hansa district of East Berlin–TAC.
United States Embassy in Athens, TAC.

1957
The Oheb Shalom Temple in Baltimore–TAC.
Senior school in Littleton, Massachusetts–TAC.
Senior school in Northfield, Massachusetts–TAC.

1958
Secondary school in Needham, Massachusetts.
Primary school in Stoughton, Massachusetts.
Two dormitories for Philips Academy in Andover, Massachusetts.
Reyim Synagogue in Newton, Massachusetts.
The Murchison house in Provincetown, Massachusetts.
Consultancy for the Pan American building in New York, with TAC and
Belluschi on the plan of Emery, Roth & Sons.

1959
Primary school in Acton, Massachusetts.
Britz-Buckow-Rudow settlement plan, with 16,000 units to house 45,000
people in West Berlin–TAC.

1960
Buildings for Brandeis University in Waltham, Massachusetts.
Senior school in Wayland, Massachusetts.
Primary school in Lincoln, Massachusetts.
Primary school at Kingston, Massachusetts.
Primary school in Waltham, Massachusetts.
Gould Hospital in Presque Isle, Maine.
Centre for blood donors at the Pediatric Hospital in Boston, Massachusetts.
Skyscraper for Grand Central Station, New York.
Shops for Sears, Roebuck & Company in Saugus, Massachusetts.

1961
Building for the J. Kennedy Federal Offices in Boston, Massachusetts–TAC.

1964
Plan for the Britz-Buckow-Rudow Centre in West Berlin–TAC.

1965
Rosenthal china factory in Selb, Germany.
University for 11,500 students, with recreational, academic, administrative
and residential buildings and a School of Medicine at Mosul, Iraq–TAC.

1967
Experimental buildings for a primary and secondary school at Britz-Buckow-
Rudow, Berlin–TAC.
Enlargement of the Huntington Art Galley.
Tower for offices, with shops, bank, restaurant and carpark for 500 cars at
Shaker Heights, Ohio–TAC.
Thomas glassworks in Hamburg.
Plan for Selb, Germany.

# Gropius's main written work

*Programm des Staatlichen Bauhauses*, 1919; *Idee und Aufbau des Staatlichen Bauhauses*,
Bauhaus publications, Weimar, 1923; *Internationale Architektur*, Bauhausbücher
n. 1, Munich, 1925; *Neue Arbeiten in Bauhauswerkstätten*, Bauhausbücher n. 7,
Munich, 1925; *Bauhausbauten in Dessau*, Bauhausbücher n. 12, Munich, 1928;
'Flach, Mittel oder Hochbau?' (speech at the Third Congress of Modern Architec-
ture in Brussels), 1930; 'Theaterbau' (speech at the Fourth Convegno Volta in
Rome), in *Atti della Reale Academia d'Italia*, 1934; 'The formal and technical
problems of Architecture and Planning' in *A.I.A. Journal*, May, 1934; 'The role
of reinforced concrete in the development of modern constructions' in *The
Concrete Way*, September–October, 1934; 'Grandes Polaciones' in *Nuestra
Arquitectura*, September, 1934; *The New Architecture and the Bauhaus*, London,
1935; 'Estratti dagli scritti di Gropius' in *Quadrante*, Milan, 1935; 'Architecture at
Harvard University' in *Architectural Records*, May, 1937; 'Essentials for creative
design' in *The Octagon*, July, 1937; 'Education towards creative design' in *American
Architects and Architecture*, May, 1937; 'Background of the new architecture' in
*Civil Engineering*, December, 1937; *Bauhaus* (written in collaboration with H.
Bayer), Museum of Modern Art, New York, 1938; 'Towards a Living Architecture' in *American architects and architecture*, January–February, 1938; 'Essentials of
architectural education' in *P.M.*, n. 42, Spring–summer, 1938; Preface to E. Denby's
book, *Europe Rehouses*, 1938; entry on 'Architecture for education' in the *Encyclopedia Britannica*, 1939; 'Training the architect' in *Twice a Year* n. 2, 1939; 'Contemporary architecture and training the architect' in *Architectural Forum*, March,

1940; 'Defense housing' (in collaboration with M. Wagner), in The Acts of Congress, *National Defence Migration*, 1941; 'Three House Types, Defense House at New Kensington' in *Architectural Forum*, October, 1941; *The new city pattern for the people and by the people*, 1942; *The problem of the cities and towns. Conference on urbanism*, Harvard University, 1942; 'Prefabrication system designed by General Panel Corporation' in *Architectural Record*, April, 1943; 'Prefabrication system designed by the General Panel Corporation' in *The New Pencil Point*, April, 1943; 'Housing in Framingham, Mass.' in *Architectural Forum*, June, 1943; 'A program for city reconstruction' in *Architectural Forum*, July, 1943; 'Variety of houses from identical prefabricated units designed by Harvard students' in *The New Pencil Point*, December, 1943; 'The architect's contribution to the post-war reconstruction' in *Bay State Builder*, 1943; 'Aluminium terrace housing, New Kensington Settlement' in *Architectural Forum*, July, 1944; 'Jewellery Shop' in *Pencil Points*, August, 1944; 'Practical field experience in building to be an integral part of an architect's training' in *Bay State Builder*, July, 1945; *Rebuilding our communities*, Chicago, 1945; 'Principles of Modern Design' in *Agnes Scott Alumnae Quarterly*, 1946; 'Design Topics', in *Magazine of Art*, December, 1947; 'Teaching the Arts of Design', in *College Art Journal*, spring, 1948; *Scope of Total Architecture*, New York, 1955.

## General works, monographs, essays

F. BLOCK, *Probleme des Bauens: Wohnbau. Walter Gropius: Der Arch. als Organisator der modernen Bauwirtsch. u. seine Forderungen an die Industrie*, Potsdam, 1928; B. TAUT, *Modern architecture*, London, 1929; M. CASTEELS, *L'art moderne primitif*, Paris, 1939; *Congrès International pour l'architecture moderne* (report), Brussels, 1930; *Internationale Kongress für neues Bauen* (report), Frankfurt, 1930; G. PLATZ, *Die Baukunst der neuesten Zeit*, Berlin, 1930; *Wasmuths Lexicon der Baukunst*, Vol. II, Berlin, 1930; S. GIEDION, *Walter Gropius*, Paris, 1931; L. ADLER, *Neuezeitliche Miethäuser und Siedlungen*, Berlin–Charlottenburg, 1931; D. ARKIN, *Modern western architecture*, Moscow, 1932; I. G. CROWTHER, *Osiris and the atom*, London, 1932; H. R. HITCHCOCK, *Modern architecture*, Museum of Modern Art, N.Y., 1932; H. R. HITCHCOCK and P. JOHNSON, *The international style: architecture since 1922*, New York, 1932; B. MORETTI, *Teatri*, Milan, 1932; M. WAGNER, *Das wachsende Haus*, Stuttgart, 1932; C. BAUER, *Modern housing*, Boston, 1934; R. MCGRATH, *Twentieth century houses*, London, 1934; H. READ, *Art and Industry*, London, 1934; A. B. BEMIS, *The evolving house. Rational design*, Vol. III, 1936; CIRCLE, *Art Education and State*, London, 1936; N. PEVSNER, *Pioneers of the modern movement*, London, 1936; W. BEHRENDT, *Modern building, its nature, problems and forms*, New York, 1937; *Walter Gropius*, edited by the Société Belge Urbanistes et Architectes, 1937; *New standard Encyclopedia of art*, New York, 1939; A. D. PICA, *Nuova architettura del monde*, Milan, 1938; *Guide to Modern Architecture*, Museum of Modern Art, New York, 1940; S. GIEDION, *Space, Time and Architecture*, Cambridge, 1941; *Built in U.S.A.*, Museum of Modern Art, New York, 1944; *Prefabricated, demontable packaged building system*, General Panel Corporation, New York, 1944; A. SARTORIS, *Gli elementi dell'architettura funzionale*, Milan, 2nd edition, 1944; B. ZEVI, *Verso un' architettura organica*, Turin, 1945; R. LODDERS, *Industriebau u. Architekt u. ihre gegenseitige Beeinflussung*, 1946; *A proposed housing program*, Reese Michael Hospital, Chicago, 1946; A. DORNER, *The way beyond 'art'*, New York, 1947; J. M. RICHARDS, *An introduction to modern architecture*, Penguin Books, 1940, reprinted 1947; E. PERSICO, *Scritti critici e polemici*, Milan, 1947; *Bicentennial conference on planning man's physical environment, Walter Gropius; In search of a common denominator of design*, Princeton University, 1947; R. LODDERS, *Von der Persönlichkeit des Architekten, Hamburg*, 1948; N. PEVSNER, *An outline of European architecture*, 2nd edition, London, 1948; RAMELLI and CASSI, *Edifici per gli spettacoli*, Milan, 1948; A. SARTORIS, *Encyclopédie de l'architecture nouvelle*, Milan, 1948; E. M. UPJOHN, WINGERT, MAHLER, *History of world art*, New York, 1948; N. PEVSNER, *Pioneers of modern design*, New York, 1949; B. ZEVI, *Saper vedere l'architettura*, Turin, 1948 (8th edition, 1970); B. ZEVI, *Storia dell'architettura moderna*, Turin, 1950 (4th edition, 1961); G. C. ARGAN, *Walter Gropius e la Bauhaus*, Turin, 1951; B. ZEVI, *Poetica dell'architettura neoplastica*, Milan, 1953; C. KURATA, *Walter Gropius*, Tokyo, 1953; S. GIEDION, *Walter Gropius, Work and Teamwork*, New York, 1954; KOKUSAI KENTIK-KYOKAY and MASAZKU KOYAMA, *Walter Gropius*, Tokyo, 1954; IWAO and MITYIKO YAMAWAKI, *Bauhaus Weimar-Dessau-Berlin*, Tokyo, 1954; L. SCHREYER, *Erinnerungen an Sturm und Bauhaus*, Munich, 1956; W. GROPIUS, *Scope of Total Architecture*, London, 1956; H. PETERS, 'Die Bauhaus-mappen' in *Neue Europäische Grafik 1921–1923*, Cologne, 1957; E. N. ROGERS, entry on 'Walter Gropius' in the *Enciclopedia Universale dell'Arte*, Vol. VI, Rome, 1958; B. ZEVI; *Architectura in nuce*, Rome, 1960 (2nd edition, Florence, 1972); G. MUCHE, *Blickpunkt Sturm, Dada, Bauhaus, Gegenwart*, Munich, 1961; *Painters of the Bauhaus*, catalogue of the exhibition at the Marlborough Galleries, London, 1962; R. MÁRTA, *A. Bauhaus és mühelyel, epités, es Közlekedéstudomàny Közlemenyek*, 1962; B. ADLER, *Das Weimarer Bauhaus*, Archive of the Bauhaus, Darmstadt, 1963; L. BENEVOLO, *Le origini dell' urbanistica moderna*, Bari, 1963; *Bauhaus-Idee-Form-Zweck-Zeit*, Catalogue of the exhibition at the Göppinger Galerie, Berlin, Frankfurt, 1964; H. WINGLER, *Die Mappen-Werk 'Neue Europäische Grafik'*, Berlin, 1965; L. LANG, *Das Bauhaus 1919–1933, Idee und Wirklichkeit*, Zentralinstitut für form Formgestaltung, Berlin, 1965; W. SCHEIDIG, *Bauhaus Weimar 1919–1924*, Munich, 1966 (English edition, London, 1966); D. SCHMIDT, *Bauhaus Weimar 1919–1925, Dessau 1925–1932, Berlin 1928–1933*, Dresden, 1966; *Les années 25, arts décos, Bauhaus, Stijl, Esprit Nouveau*, in the catalogue of the exhibition at the Musée des Arts Decoratifs, Paris, 1966; L. BENEVOLO, *Storia dell'architettura moderna*, Bari, 1966; *Bauhaus–a teaching idea*, in the catalogue of the exhibition at the Carpenter Center for the Visual Arts, Harvard University, 1967; *Bauhaus*, in the catalogue of the exhibition at the Staatliche Galerie Schloss Georgium, Dessau, 1967; G. NAYLOR, *Bauhaus*, London, 1968; *Bauhaus 1919–1969*, catalogue of the exhibition at the Musée National d'Art Moderne, Paris, April–June, 1969; E. PIRODDI, entry on Walter Gropius' in the *Dizionario Enciclopedico di Architettura e Urbanistica*, Vol. III, Rome, 1969; G. C. ARGAN, *L'arte moderna 1770–1970*, Florence, 1970; B. ZEVI, *Cronache di architettura*, Bari, 1970–1971.

## Essays, drawings and plans published in reviews.

'Das Bürohaus von W. Gropius' (Werkbund-Ausstellung) in *Kunstgewerbeblatt, neue Folge*, Vol. 26, p. 44, 1915; 'Kunstpolitik, der Geist von Weimar' in *Cicerone*, Vol. 13, p. 186, 1921; A. BEHNE, 'Entwürfe und Bauten von W. Gropius' in *Centralblatt der Bauverwaltung*, Vol. 42, pp. 637–640, 1922; 'Corrispondenza dalla Germania' in *Architettura e Arti decorative*, Vol. 2, pp. 496–501, 1922–1923; H. G. SCHEFFAUER, 'Building the master-builder: the Bauhaus of Weimar' in *Freeman*, Vol. 8, pp. 304–305, New York, 1923; Id., 'The work of W. Gropius' in *Architectural Review*, Vol. 56, pp. 50–54, 1924; 'Developpement de l'esprit architectural moderne en Allemagne' in *Esprit Nouveau*, n. 27, 1924; W. GROPIUS, 'Baugeist d. neuen Volksgemeinde' in *Glocke*, Vol. 10, p. 311, Berlin, 1924; Id., 'Grundziele d. Staatl. Bauhauses' in *Hilfe*, p. 226, Berlin, 1924; Id., 'Bauhaus' in *Vivos Voco*, pp. 11–16, 1924; 'Faguswerke, Alfeld an der Leine' in *Wasmuths Monatshefte für Baukunst*, Vol. 7, nos. 1–2, pp. 48–50, 1924; W. GROPIUS, 'Wie wollen wir in Zukunft bauen?' in *Wohnungsfürsorge*, Vol. 5, p. 152, Vienna, 1924; Id., 'Neue Bau Gesinnung' in *Innendekoration*, Vol. 36, p. 134, Darmstadt, 1925; Id., 'Bauplan fur d. neue Frdr-Fröbel-Haus' in *Kindergarten*, Vol. 66, pp. 27–39, Weimar, 1925; Id., 'Grundsätze d. Bauhausproduktion' in *Neue Erziehung*, Vol. 6, p. 656, Berlin, 1925; Id., 'Grundlinien für neues Bauen' in *Bau und Werkkunst*, pp. 13–47, 1926; 'Das flache Dach', in *Bauwelt*, Vol. 17, pp. 162–168, 223–227 and 361, Berlin, 1926; W. GROPIUS, 'Grundsätze d. Bauhausprodukt' in *Vivos Voco*, pp. 265–267, 1926; Id., 'Grundsätze d. Bauhausprodukt', in *Werkland* (Vivos Voco), Vol. 4, pp. 265–267, Leipzig, 1926; Id., 'Wie bauen wir billigere, bessere, schöne Wohnungen' in *Werkland*, (Vivos Voco), Vol. 4, p. 268, Leipzig, 1926; P. LINDER, 'El nuevo Bauhaus en Dessau' in *Arquitectura*, Vol. 9, pp. 110–112, 1927; W. GROPIUS, 'Wirtschaftlichkeit neuer Baumethoden' in *Bauamt und Gemeindebau*, Hanover, 1927; Id., 'Trocken Bauweise' in *Baugilde*, Vol. 9, p. 1362, Berlin, 1927; Id., 'Systemat, Vorarbeit f. rationellen Wohnungsbau' in *Bauwelt*, Vol. 18, p. 197, Berlin, 1927; Id., 'Rationalisierg. d. Bauwirtsch.' in *Bund*, Berne, 1927; Id., 'Zum Streit um d. flache Dach' in *Stein, Holz, Eisen*, Vol. 41, pp. 125, 129, 191, Frankfurt, 1927; Id., 'Normung und Wohnungsnot' in *Technik und Wirtschaft*, Vol. 20, p. 7, 1927; Id., 'Geistige u. techn. Voraussetzg. d. neuen Baukunst' in *Umschau*, Vol. 31, p. 909, Frankfurt, 1927; Id., 'Bauhaus in Dessau Der Aufgang' in *Velhagen und Klasings Monatshefte*, Vol. 41, pp. 86–90, Leipzig, 1927; P. F. SCHMIDT, 'Vom Dessauer Bauhaus' in *Westermans Monatshefte*, Vol. 142, pp. 179–184, 1927; 'Dernières oeuvres de Walter Gropius' in *Cahiers d'Art*, Vol. 2, pp. 118–120, 1927; W. GROPIUS, 'D. Grosse Baukasten' in *Neue Frankfurt*, I–II, pp. 25–30, Frankfurt, 1927–1928; Id., 'Bauen und Wohnen' in *Baugilde*, Vol. 10, p. 1313, Berlin, 1928; Id., 'Ergebnis d. Reichsforschung' in *Bauwelt*, Vol. 20, pp. 158–162, Berlin, 1928; Id., 'Staffelg, d. Energien. Von d. neuen Einstellg. Z. Arbeit' in *Innendekoration*, Vol. 39, p. 478, Darmstadt, 1928; Id., 'Der Architekt als Organisat. d. mod. Bauwirtsch.' in *Kreis*, Vol. 4, pp. 119–122, Hamburg, 1928; Id., 'Mod. Theaterbau unt. Berücks d. Piscator Theaterneubaues in Berlin' in *Scene*, Vol. 18, p. 4, Charlottenburg 1928; Id., 'Stadtkrone f. Halle a. S.' in *Stein, Holz, Eisen*, Vol. 42, pp. 832–837, Frankfurt, 1928; 'Walter Gropius und d. Dessauer Bauhaus' in *Wasmuths Monatshefte für Baukunst*, Vol. 12, p. 100, 1928; 'Totaltheater' in *Moderne Bauformen*, Vol. 27, pp. 340–341, 1928; W. GROPIUS, 'Bebauungspl. und Wohnformen d. Dammerstock Siedlung' in *Baugilde*, Vol. 11, p. 1658, Berlin, 1929, Id., 'Nichteisenmetall, die Baustoffe d. Zukunft' in *Metallwirtschaft*, Vol. 8, pp. 89–91, Berlin, 1929; Id., 'Entwurf für die Forschungsiedlung Spandau-Haselhorst' in *Städtbau*, Vol. 24, pp. 89–90, 1929; 'Dammerstock Siedlung' in *Bauwarte*, Vol. 5, pp. 385–395 and 437–451, Cologne, 1929; E. A. HORNER, 'Modern Architecture in Germany' in *Architectural Forum*, Vol. 51, pp. 41 and ff., 1929; W. GROPIUS, 'Wohnformen: flach-, mittel-u. Hochbau?' in *Neue Berlin*, pp. 74–80, Berlin, 1930; 'Totaltheater' in *Architectural Record*, Vol. 67, pp. 492–494, 1930; P. LINDER, 'Walter Gropius' in *Arquitectura*, Vol. 12, pp. 245–254, 1930; TURKEL-DERI, 'Exhibition of architectural designs' in *Art News*, Vol. 28, p. 14, 1930; S. GIEDION, 'Walter Gropius et l'architecture en Allemagne' in *Cahiers d'Art*, Vol. 50, pp. 95–103, 1930; 'Walter Gropius' in *Cicerone*, Vol. 22, pp. 17–18, 469–475 and suppl. 59–60, 1930; W. GROPIUS, 'Small houses of today' in *Architectural Forum*, Vol. 54, pp. 266–278, 1931; Id., 'Was erhoffen wir vom russ. Städtebau' in *Neue Russland*, Vol. 8, pp. 57–61, Berlin, 1931; Id., 'Was erwartet d. mod. Architekt von d. Baustoffchemie?' in *Zeitschrift für Angewandte Chemie*, Vol. 44, pp. 765–768, Berlin, 1931; J. BALDOVICI, 'L'oeuvre architecturale de Walter Gropius' in *Architecture Vivante*, Vol. 9, pp. 28–29, 1931; 'Conferencia de Walter Gropius en la residencia de los estudiantes de Madrid' in *Arquitectura*, Vol. 13, pp. 50–52, 1931; 'Kharkov, National Theater Competition' in *Deutsche Bauzeitung*, Vol. 65, pp. 66 and ff., 1931; 'Berlin, Siemensstadt Housing' in *Housing and Building*, Vol. 3, nos. 1–2, 1931; 'Neue Wohnungsprojekte von prof. Gropius' in *Werk*, Vol. 18, pp. 121–128, Zurich, 1931; PORCHER, 'Walter Gropius et l'architecture moderne' in *Art et Decoration*, Vol. 59, pp. 21–32, 1931; I. PANNAGGI, 'Walter Gropius' in *Casabella*, n. 50, 1932; Id., 'Il Teatro Total' in *Scenario*, Vol. 1, n. 6, Milan, 1932; 'Berlin building exhibition of 1931. Cooperative apartment' in *T. Square*, Vol. 2, 1932; W. GROPIUS, 'Formal and technical problems of modern architecture and planning' in *Royal Institute of British Architects Journal*, Vol. 41, pp. 679–694, 1934; Id., 'Rehousing in big cities–outwards or upwards?' in *The Listener*, Vol. 11, pp. 814–816, London, 1934; 'Opening of the Gropius exhibition', in *RIBA Journal*, Vol. 41, p. 703, 1934; P. M. SHAND, 'Scenario for a human drama: immediate background' in *Architectural Review*, Vol. 76, p. 42, 1934; J. M. RICHARDS, 'Walter Gropius' in *Architectural Review*, Vol. 78, pp. 44–46, 1935; 'Cry stop to havoc; or, Preservation by concentrated development; scheme for a block of flats at Windsor' in *Architectural Review*, Vol. 77, pp. 188–192, 1935; 'Chelsea–House in Church St.' in *Architectural Review*, Vol. 80, pp. 249–253, 1936; 'Chelsea, Two houses in Church St.' in *Architects Journal*, Vol. 84, pp. 869–871, 1936; 'Exhibit in a conference room for a corporation' in *Architectural Record*, Vol. 80, pp. 426–427, 1936; G. NELSON, 'Architects of Europe today, Walter Gropius' in *Pencil Point*, Vol. 17, pp. 422–432, 1936; W. GROPIUS, 'Background of the new architecture' in *Civil Engineering*, Vol. 7, pp. 839–842, 1937; Id., 'Incontro all 'America' in *Casabella*, Vol. 120, p. 6, 1937; 'Harvard engage famed architects' in *Boston Herald-Traveller*, 25 January, 1937; W. DOOLEY, 'Gropius brings modernism to Harvard' in *Boston Evening Transcript*, 28 January, 1937; 'Bauhaus man' in *Time*, New York, 8 February, 1937; 'A modernist scans our skyline; Gropius, German architect bound for Harvard sees an original style emerging in America' in *New York Times Magazine*, 11 April, 1937; 'Architecture at Harvard University' in *Architectural Record*, Vol. 81, pp. 8–11, 1937; 'Villa a Chelsea' in *Casabella*, vol. 109, pp. 1 and 32–33, 1937; 'Gropius to Harvard' in *Architectural Forum*, Vol. 66, 1937; 'Papworth. Village College' in *Architects Journal*, Vol. 86, p. 705; 1937; 'Chelsea house' in *Architects Journal*, Vol. 86, pp. 263–264, 337–338, 409–410 and 547–548, 1937; 'London, Mortimer Gallery, electrical centre' in *Architects Journal*, Vol. 86, pp. 229–230, 1937; 'The new Bauhaus in Chicago' in *Current History*, Vol. 47, pp. 90–92, 1937; 'Education toward creative design', in *American Architecture*, Vol. 150, 1937; 'Progressive Triumph' in *Magazine of Art*, Vol. 30, p. 186, 1937; W. GROPIUS, 'Essentials for architectural education' in *PM, An Intimate Journal for Production Managers*, Vol. 4, n. 5, pp. 3–16, 1938; Id., 'Towards a living Architecture' (Japanese translation), in *Kokusai-Kentiku*, Vol. 14, pp. 105–107, 1938; 'Contrast at Harvard' in *Time*, New York, 11 April, 1938; 'Casa nel Kent' in *Casabella*, Vol. 123, pp. 36–37, 1938; 'Wheaton Art Center', in *Casabella*, Vol. 130, pp. 32–33, 1938; 'Kent. Timber House', in *Architectural Review*, Vol. 83, pp. 61–63, 1938; 'Wheaton College art center, design and plans' in *Architectural Forum*, Vol. 69, pp. 148–149, 1938; 'Impington Village College, model, plans, details' in *Architects Journal*, Vol. 87, pp. 590–591, 1938; 'Cambridge. Christ's College, proposed new building plans, perspectives, elevations' in *Architects Journal*, Vol. 87, pp. 202–203, 241, 1938; 'Sevenoaks. House' in *Architects Journal*, Vol. 88, pp. 285–286, 1938; 'Towards a living architecture' in *American Architect*, Vol. 152, 1938; G. H. PERKINS, 'Walter Gropius' (with introduction by H. R. HITCHCOCK), in *Shelter*, Vol. 3, n. 2, 1938; 'Gropius: house at Lincoln' in *Focus*, n. 2, pp. 16–19, 1938; L. MOHOLY-NAGY, 'Education and the Bauhaus' in *Focus*, n. 2, pp. 20–27, 1938; W. GROPIUS, 'Training the architect' in *Twice a Year*, n. 2, pp. 142–151, 1939; 'Cohasset and Lincoln houses' in *Architectural Review*, Vol. 86, pp. 189–194, 1939; 'Impington Village College' *Architectural Review*, Vol. 86, pp. 227–234, 1939; 'Impington Village College' in *Architecture d'Aujourd'hui*, Vol. 10, pp. 28–29, 1939; 'Lincoln House for Walter Gropius' in *Architectural Forum*, Vol. 71, pp. 28–31, 1939; 'Lincoln House for Breuer' in *Architectural Forum*, Vol. 71, pp. 455–459, 1939; 'Lincoln. Ford house' in *House Beautiful*, Vol. 81, pp. 41–43, 1939; 'Lincoln. Ford house' in *Architectural Record*, Vol. 87, pp. 108–111, 1940; 'Cohasset Beach. Hagerty House' in *Architectural Forum*, Vol. 72, pp. 295–303, 1940; 'Cohasset. Hagerty House', in *Kokusai-Kentiku*, vol. 16, pp. 128–129, 1940; 'Lincoln. Breuer and Ford House' in *Kokuasi-Kentiku*, Vol. 16, pp. 130–133, 1940; W. GROPIUS, 'Training the architect for contemporary architecture', in *National Education Association. Department of Art Education Bulletin*, Vol. 7, pp. 137–146, 1941; 'Pittsburg House' in *Architectural Forum*, Vol. 74, pp. 160–170, 1941; 'New Kensington defence houses' in *Architectural Forum*, Vol. 75, pp. 218–220, 1941; 'Impington Village College' in *Architectural Journal*, Vol. 94, pp. 237, 245–248, 1941; 'Profile of a dreamer who makes his dreams bloom into reality' in *Boston Herald*, 14 June, 1942; 'Wayland House' in *Architectural Forum*, Vol. 77, pp. 76–77, 1942; 'Recreational center proposed for Key West' in *Architectural Forum*, Vol. 77, pp. 83–85, 1942; 'Dessau. House of Walter Gropius' in *South African Architectural Record*, Vol. 27, p. 21, 1942; W. GROPIUS, 'The architect's contribution to the post-war construction program' in *Bay State Builder*, Vol. 1, pp. 27–30 and 36–37, 1943; 'Framingham House' in *Architectural Forum*, Vol. 78, pp. 77–79, 1943; W. GROPIUS and M. WAGNER, 'Program for city reconstruction' in *Architectural Forum*, Vol. 79, pp. 75–86, 1943; 'New Kensington. Aluminium City terrace housing' in *Architectural Forum*, Vol. 81, pp. 65–76, 1943; H. HERREY, 'Prefabricated system for architects' in *Pencil Point*, Vol. 24, pp. 36–47, 1943; 'houses from identical prefabricated units' in *Pencil Point*, Vol. 24, pp. 76–81, 1943; 'Prefabricated panels for packaged building developed by E. Wachsmann and W. Gropius' in *Architectural Record*, Vol. 93, pp. 50–53, 1943; 'Framingham. House' in *Architects Journal*, Vol. 98, pp. 187–188, 1943; 'Packaged building' in *Interiors*, Vol. 103, pp. 38–41, 1943; S. MOLLI, 'Considerazioni sulla teoria di Walter Gropius circa le altezze delle case' in *Urbanistica*, Vol. 12, pp. 15–17, 1943; 'Small houses of the future' in *Celotex News*, October, 1943; 'Jewelry shop by Walter Gropius' in *Pencil Point*, Vol. 25, pp. 54–55, 1944; 'Three student solutions to a church design problem conducted at Harvard University' in *Pencil Point*, Vol. 25, pp. 75–78, 1944; 'New Kensington. Wartime housing estate in Pennsylvania' in *Architectural Review*, Vol. 96, pp. 72–76, 1944; 'Expansible prefabricated house for postwar' in *Architectural Record*, Vol. 96, p. 69, 1944; 'Wayland. Chamberlain house' in *House and Garden*, Vol. 87, p. 62, 1944; 'City planning theories defended', in *New York Times Magazine*, 9 July, 1944; 'Gropius vision post-war building boom using prefabricated component parts' in *Harvard Crimson*, 20 October, 1944; 'General Panel Corporation cloisons démontables' in *Techniques et Architecture*, Vol. 5, nos. 5–6, 1945; 'Field experience and the making of an architect' in *American Institute of Architects Journal*, Vol. 4, pp. 210–212, November, 1945; 'Willimantic: proposed public library' in *Arts and Architecture*, Vol. 63, pp. 28–29, 1946; 'A hospital plan' in *Architectural Forum*, vol. 85, pp. 87–104, 1946; 'Living architecture or international style?' in *Design*, Vol. 47, pp. 10–11, 1946; 'Walter Gropius y Marcel Breuer' in *Nuestra Arquitectura*, n. 12, pp. 414–427, 1946; 'New Kensington Pa, Aluminium City' in *Architecture d'Aujourd'hui*, Vol. 18, p. 31, 1947; 'Le système de préfabrication de la General Panel Corporation' in *L'Architecture d'Aujourd'hui*, Vol. 18, pp. 95–98, 1947; 'Leader on prefabricated housing' in *New York Times Magazine*, 2 March, 1947; 'On basic philosophy for artists' in *New York Times Magazine*, 27 April, 1947; 'Says U.S. expected Foreign Mins, Council breakdown; reports plan to rebuild Frankfurt' in *New York Times Magazine*, 17 December 1947; 'House in industry: a system for the manufacture of industrialized building elements by Gropius and Wachsmann for the General Panel Corporation' in *Arts and Architecture*, Vol. 64, pp. 38–47, 1947; 'The industrialized house: General Panel Corporation' in *Architectural Forum*, Vol. 86, pp. 115–120, 1947; 'Urbanism' (lecture by W.G.), in *Architects Journal*, Vol. 106, pp. 276–277, 1947; W. GROPIUS, 'Design Topics', in *Magazine of Art*, Vol. 40, pp. 298–304, 1947; UNO and the architects (comment by W.G.), in *Architect and Building News*, Vol. 190, p. 232, 1947; 'Frank letter to J. D. Leland' in *American Institute of Architects Journal*, Vol. 7, pp. 198–202, April, 1947; 'Impington Village College', in *Werk*, Vol. 34, p. 117, 1947; W. GROPIUS, 'Teaching the arts of design' in *College Art Journal*, Vol. 7, pp. 160–164, 1948; Id., 'Reconstruction: Germany' in *Task*, nos. 7–8, pp. 134–135, 1948; 'Will Europe build cities or shanty towns?' in *Weekend*, January, 1948; 'Walter Gropius spricht über Städtebau' (speech to the C.I.A.M. in 1947), in *Aufbau*, Vol. 3, pp. 83–84, 1948; M. WAGNER, 'Die Stadtschaft auf dem Reissbrett' in *Bauen und Wohnen*, Vol. 3, 1948; 'In search of a new monumentality' in *Architectural Review*, Vol. 104, pp. 117–122, 1948; 'Maison de Vacance à Wayland' in *L'Architecture d'Aujourd'hui*, Vol. 19, pp. 6–7, 1948; 'Maison de Breuer à Lincoln' in *L'Architecture d'Aujourd'hui*, Vol. 19, pp. 10–12, 1948; 'Made Designers for industry of the Royal Society of Arts' in *Architectural Forum*, Vol. 88, p. 14, 1948; 'Harvard will build 3 million worth of functional dormitories', in *Architectural Forum*, Vol. 89, p. 15, 1948; 'Greensboro, N.C. Plant of Container Corporation of America' in *Architectural Forum*, Vol. 89, pp. 90–95, 1948; 'Sobre planeamento del mundo circundante humano' in *Revista de Arquitectura*, Vol. 33, pp. 4–7, 1948; 'Casa en Lincoln' in *Revista de Arquitectura*, Vol. 33, p. 223, 1948; 'Harvard reaffirms an old tradition: proposed Graduate Center', in *Architectural Record*, Vol. 104, p. 118, 1948; W. GROPIUS, 'Organic neighborhood planning' in *Housing and Town and Country Planning Bulletin*, n. 2, pp. 2–5, 1949; B. ADLER, 'The Bauhaus 1919–1933' in *The Listener*, Vol. 41, pp. 485–486, London, 1949; N. PEVSNER, 'From William Morris to Walter Gropius' in *The Listener*, Vol. 41, p. 439, London, 1949; J. L. MARTIN, 'The Bauhaus and its influence' in *The Listener*, Vol. 41, pp. 527–529, London, 1949; 'The design that Cambridge rejected, the Gropius-Fry scheme for Christ's College' in *Architects Journal*, Vol. 109, p. 116, 1949; 'Cambridge, Massachusetts, Harvard University. Graduate Center plans, views of model' in *Architects Journal*, Vol. 109, pp. 125–126, 1949; 'Flexibility at Harvard: two-man dormitory room of the proposed Harvard Graduate Center' in *Architectural Forum*, Vol. 90, p. 36, 1949; 'Lincoln. Gropius house' in *House and Garden*, Vol. 95, pp. 72–77, 112, 114, 115–117, 1949; 'Walter Gropius et son école' special number of *L'Architecture d'Aujourd'hui*, 28, 1950; JOHN A. THWAITES, 'Bauhaus painters and the new style epoch' in *Art Quarterly*, 14th year, pp. 19–32, 1951; M. BILL, 'The Bauhaus idea' in *The Architects yearbook*, n. 5, pp. 29–32, 1953; E. BERGEN, '3 Bauhaus' in *De Nevelvlek*, 1956; W. GROHMANN, 'Bauhaus' in *L'Oeil*, n. 28, Paris, April, 1957; M. GOLDRING, 'The Bauhaus–30 years after' in *3 Architectural design*, Vol. 28, 1958; S. MOHOLY-NAGY, 'Bauhaus and modern typography' in *Print*, 4th year, pp. 45–48, 1960; 'Bauhaus' in the *Catalogue of the travelling exhibition, Kunsthalle, Darmstadt*, 1961; 'The Bauhaus, aspects and influence' in the *Catalogue of Gallery A., Melbourne*, 1961; W. VON ECKART, 'The Bauhaus', in *Horizon*, Vol. 4, n. 2, pp. 58–77, November, 1961; L. GROTE, 'Zum Gestaltwandel des Bauhauses' in *Die Kunst*, 1961; H. BREDENDIECK, 'The legend of the Bauhaus' in *Art Journal*, 22nd year, pp. 15–21, 1962; H. DEARSTYNE, 'Bauhaus revisited', in *Journal of the American Institute of Architects*, 38th year, pp. 79–82, 1962; S. GIEDION, 'Das Bauhaus and seine Zeit' in *Bau und Werk*, 15th year, pp. 59–60, 1962; N. LYNTON, 'The Bauhaus in perspective' in *Impulse*, n. 21, 1962; 'W. Gropius' in *Journal of the American Institute of Architects*, pp. 120–122, 1963; N. A. BOWMAN, 'Bauhaus influence on an evolving theatre architecture, some development stages' in *Theatre Survey*, Vol. 6, n. 2, 1965; E. NEUMANN, 'Typographie, Grafik und Werbung am Bauhaus' in *Neue Grafik*, nos. 17–18, 1965; E. ROTERS, 'Maler am Bauhaus' in *Die Kunst unserer Zeit*, Vol. 18, Berlin, 1965; H. WINGLER, 'Origine et Histoire du Bauhaus' in *Cahiers Renaud-Barrault*, February, 1966; Id., 'Das Bauhaus 1919–1933', Rasch, Bramsche, 1962 (2nd edition revised and completed in 1968, published in English by the M.I.T. Press, Mass., 1968).

'The Bauhaus, aspects and influence' in the *Catalogue of Gallery A., Melbourne*, 1961; W. VON ECKART, 'The Bauhaus', in *Horizon*, Vol. 4, n. 2, pp. 58–77, November, 1961; L. GROTE, 'Zum Gestaltffiandel des Bauhauses' in *Die Kunst*, 1961; H. BREDENDIECK, 'The legend of the Bauhaus' in *Art Journal*, 22nd year, pp. 15–21, 1962; H. DEARSTYNE, 'Bauhaus revisited', in *Journal of the American Institute of Architects*, 38th year, pp. 79–82, 1962; S. GIEDION, 'Das Bauhaus and seine Zeit' in *Bau und Werk*, 15th year, pp. 59–60, 1962; N. LYNTON, 'The Bauhaus in perspective' in *Impulse*, n. 21, 1962; W. Gropius' in *Journal of the American Institute of Architects*, pp. 120–122, 1963; N. A. BOWMAN, 'Bauhaus influence on an evolving theatre architecture, some development stages' in *Theatre Survey*, Vol. 6, n. 2, 1965; E. NEUMANN, 'Typographie, grafik und werbung am Bauhaus' in *Neue Grafik*, nos. 17–18, 1965; E. ROTERS, 'Maler am Bauhaus' in *Die Kunst unserer Zeit*, Vol. 18, Berlin, 1965; H. WINGLER, 'Origine et Histoire du Bauhaus' in *Cahiers Renaud-Barrault*, February, 1966; Id., 'Das Bauhaus 1919–1933', Nasch, Bramsche, 1962 (2nd edition revised and completed in 1968, published in English by the M.I.T. Press, Mass., 1968).

APP